Financial Secrets of the Ages

Understanding How Money Flows

Dr. David E. Fritsche Sr.

Financial Secrets of the Ages

Copyright © 2010 by Dynamix Worx

ISBN-13: 978-1456451486

ISBN-10: 1456451480

Dynamix Worx
Publications

Dedication

To "THEY."

They have promised to take care of us, but failed. They were expected to show up in time to make a difference, but they did not.

They, we assumed, were smart enough to know what was about to happen, but they did not.

- They made promises they did not keep.
- They are the most unreliable group on earth, and yet we keep trying to get them to do what we expect them to do.
- They are a complete and utter failure, accomplishing nothing we are told they will do and not even bothering to let us know.

"They!"

They have wasted our time and energy in expecting, waiting, presuming, hoping, and assuming. But they have brought to us one very important truth that we would not understand without them -

"They" do not exist!

So, now we can forget them and get started doing for ourselves what they cannot, will not and should not!

To "They!"

Table of Contents

WARNING –

1. This book will challenge your thinking. You will disagree with some of it, and you will have emotional reactions to that disagreement. That is OK. I give you permission to disagree. Yet, I warn you, I will not avoid the message to accommodate your reaction. You will have to evaluate that emotion, deal with your fear and decide whether to change your view of things or not.

2. I am a theologian. In some politically correct circles it is not popular to be religious, particularly Christian. I warn you ahead of time. I am a Christian and much of my world view is influenced by my studies and concepts of God. If you object to that, you might want to read something else. If you wish to continue, please understand that I have no illusions that I will, by writing a few lines of ink on paper, alter your religious perspective. That is not my point. The point is, I will arrive at some of my conclusions through a matrix of religious philosophy. If you can journey with me on that path, agree or not, then please come on this journey.

3. I will be presenting either/or alternative concepts that will press you to make decisions. In the belief that how one believes either releases the world to us or restricts the world from us, you may have to make up your mind about concepts with which you have not had to deal before. While some will find that prospect exciting and adventurous, some will recoil and want to avoid the internal conflict.

4. The secrets revealed will not necessarily make you

comfortable. They will however, challenge you to change and to rethink your view of reality. If you are open to that challenge than you are ready for an adventure into critical thinking about some important and exciting concepts that will release you to the world around you as never before.

So, get on board, and let's venture into our world of revelation. Let's open ourselves to understanding for the first time, that the world is not flat – so to speak.

The Author

Introduction

Yes, I do believe in secrets.

The world was flat for all of human history until **Nicolaus Copernicus** (February 19, 1473 – May 24, 1543) popularized his theories of the universe. Although there were others who precede his findings of the universe, it took thousands of years to build an intellectual context in which the fact that the earth is spherical could be understood and accepted.

Such is the case with much of the history of human discovery. We travel through time and space, locked into our own ignorance, assuming certain things that are not true and which limit our world. The secret that liberates us from that ignorance is hidden behind layers of tradition, folk lore and assumptions and we do not know to challenge or to think critically about because there is no impelling need and no context in which to understand.

Human discovery and progress is found in the occasional discovery of something that is mind blowing in that it could not be understood until the context for its understanding is developed and the stage is set for its emergence into the world of reality. Even then, skeptics will always be present to keep shouting the misunderstandings of the past.

I remember the news reports of man walking on the moon. It was revolutionary and wonderful, but there were some who could not get their mind around it. They proposed that the pictures were staged in a studio somewhere, because man could not do such a thing. God, they thought, would not permit man to go beyond the bounds of earth.

Such is the contrast and conflict with all revelation where a new view of our world and of reality reveals the ignorance of the past. This process of discovery has not only brought us through the enlightenment and into the scientific age of mega revelation, but has given rise to a rush of revolutionary understanding that is changing our world daily. The sheer volume of new information is increasing at such a pace that it is impossible to grasp it all. Not only is the process of understanding happening but the pace of it is becoming increasingly shortened in time. It took thousands of years to discover that the world was not flat. It then took us a few hundred year until Einstein told us that time is not strictly linear.

And yet, with all of the wonderful discoveries of modern times, much of our world continues with the mind set and emotions of past generations, languishing in poverty, sickness and pain. While modern medical science has yet to discover a cure for AIDS, it has discovered management systems that is limiting its affects on those who have it. Yet, whole continents have not embraced the knowledge that will set them free and continue in the agony of increasing death rates.

While abundance is the general profile of our nation and most of Europe, there are still parts of our world that are steeped in restrictive economic policies and world views that tend to poverty, pollution and lack of freedom, both politically and financially. Wars are being fought because of conflicting world views and resentment of progress.

I invite you to come with me into a critical analysis of some of the secrets of our world and how it operates. There is a direct correlation between our perspective of reality and the future that we create. Poverty is not a state that overtakes us while we are unaware. It is the result of a mind set. It is a way of thinking. If we can change our world view, we can change our lives. What we are and what we have is not the mysterious function of the hidden laws of fate. It is the end result of how we believe, how we act and how we see our world and how it operates.

Chapter One

How we view money

I walked into the convention center in a daze. The lights glistened on the shiny fresh paint of new cars. The hall bustled with the activities of intense businessmen in new suits, fine shoes, and grand intentions. This annual convention of General Motors Automobile Dealers was set in a palatial hall that rivaled the Taj Mahal. Its purpose was to announce the new vehicle models, their new horns, whistles, and gadgets. It was splendid, with open bars scattered throughout the hall and hors d'oeuvres in splendor and volume, enough to feed nations. The program was grand, the orchestra magnificent, and I was miserable.

Just two weeks before I had been unemployed. The business I had worked hard to create had been squandered away by a trusted partner. I had been left destitute, without enough money to get through another month.

Answering an ad in the newspaper, I went to an obscure office in a high rise building in Los Angeles and walked out dizzied by what had happened. I went in to apply for a job that was not described in the ad, for a company that was similarly not apparent. I walked out with a new car, full insurance benefits, stock options, expense account, and a salary that was beyond my wildest expectations. Two weeks later I was in the best hotel in Detroit entertaining people who had more money than I could count. And, I was miserable.

I was miserable because I had not yet become oriented to the social climate and because of the hors d'oeuvres. Yes, the hors d'oeuvres. Not that I didn't enjoy them; food has never been

11

something that I avoid well. But the quality and quantity was a reflection of the money spent on the whole production. It was elaborate, expensive and, to my mentality, somewhere close to obscene. I reacted.

I was raised by a loving father and mother who gave their all to see that we had clothes and food and a Christian heritage. Dad pastored several small churches in rural communities and worked to support the family while pastoring. I admired his dedication and diligence. I still do. It was in this setting that I met and married Linda, the most beautiful girl I had ever seen. She attended the church that Dad pastored with her family. We had little, but they had nothing. They traveled in the summer, following the harvests in California's Central Valley, with everything they owned in the family car. We were the products of parents who bore the scars of poverty and they trained us to be frugal in our use of money.

So there I stood, surrounded by millionaires, eating delicacies that would titillate the palates of kings, but I could not relate. I was out of my league. Somehow it all seemed both unreal and immoral. It was unreal in that I had never experienced such wealth, and immoral in that this seemed to be such a waste of resources. I had seen the resentment of many in our social groups toward the rich and famous, but I had discarded it as envy, self-justification, and immaturity. Now I was faced with an internal dilemma of my own: could I reorient my sense of worth and values to accommodate this new world of finance, or was I doomed to a head-on conflict with Mammon?

In the following four years my whole perspective of God, the world and myself changed. I questioned my roots, my theology of money, and my sense of value. This book is the result of that revolution.

I began to ask:

- Does money corrupt people's values and attitudes? Why do these people with money think differently than I do?
- Does this different attitude and sense of value attract money? Which comes first, the money or the way these people view it?
- Can value be created or is there a limited supply? Does one person, having a lot of money, deprive me and others, of having our fair share?
- Is money evil and why does it flow to certain places and not to others?

The subject of money is a point of controversy in many circles. It shouldn't be. Jesus used parables dealing with money more than any other single item. But just as there are people with money in our world and  people without, that same dichotomy exists within our world. Whole church movements propose that everyone should be rich and that somehow our monetary worth verifies our spirituality. And others propose exactly the opposite: that true spirituality is established in our having nothing and living in simplicity. There are extremes on both sides that measure us and our level of success by the financial context we choose. Both are extreme, both are in error, and are equal opposites of the other.

Seminars are springing up everywhere, covering money issues. Books and tapes about money proliferate our bookshelves. Some proclaim that our economy is going to collapse and encourage us to accept a survival mentality. Others suggest that we should live in a type of Communalism with no personal possessions. Thousands of voices, each with a position to sell, call for our allegiance, and more, for our money. The television blasts out the plight of the poor, and declares the need for another poverty program, projecting the tension of immediate crisis. We are told of starving nations, for which we are responsible, and led to a sense of guilt and embarrassment for our level of income. We learn to not listen. We turn off the TV; throw away the unopened mail appeals, and go off to work, only to be faced again with the issue of money.

How can we relate to this money issue? That was my question. The following is my current answer. I do not assume that it is adequate for every time, person or situation. Over time, further revelation (that I believe for and expect in every arena of my life) may show this answer to be inadequate. But for now, it is a comfortable foundation that has released me from guilt, to be able to give more than ever before, and to live in harmony with both our childhood poverty and our present challenges.

Chapter Two

Secret #1 - There Are No Limits

The population of the planet is now over 6.5 billion according to the U. S. Census Bureau. It is projected to grow to over 9.2 billion by the year 2050. That is almost a 50% jump in 43 years.

But look at the past estimates of population on the planet. In the year of 1000 BC there were approximately 50 million people. We have gained some 6,450,000,000 people since then.

If you have read history to any degree you will remember the mention of famine, pestilence, and of the trials of man wrestling with the resource of the planet to meet the need of mere existence. How is it that this planet had trouble supporting fifty million people, but generations later seems to have less trouble supporting six and a half billion?

The process of accomplishing this task has necessitated some changes in our way of doing things.

First, we have had to conquer some diseases that threatened to reduce the population of the human race to extinction.

Second, we have had to alter our management of the earth's productivity. Where the tribal nomad used up the available supply of food and moved on in search of more, we have developed an agricultural management style of living in which we stay on the land, plant and harvest. That is a major shift in our concepts of supply and demand and has increased productivity enormously.

Third! The next great advancement in agricultural resource management was the development of irrigation, so that man is not as dependent on the shifting patterns of nature. Rather than wait for the water, we have learned how to deliver the water to the crop and thus to control the environment of production.

The same is true of any of the human needs that we can mention. Clothing, tools, the agricultural process, transportation, marketing, packaging, preservation, nutritional content, - all have undergone a major revolution that allows man to manage the planet and control its production.

But what of the non-renewable resources that we are so dependent on. What of natural gas, coal, crude oil, and other minerals that simply exist and cannot be re-grown with each harvest?

There are thousands of dilemmas in our world, that can strike fear and terror into our hearts and minds about the future, but rest assured, we are not short of resources – never have been. The problem is not with the confines of limited resources but on the lack of creativeness and ingenuity. Human history did not happen easily with resources sprouting from the ground, but by the ingenious ideas that find the resources and create ways of putting them into use.

The fears that we would run out of resources have proven unfounded. We have far more people living far better today than ever in human history. We have accomplished this by rethinking what we do and how we do it. We have accomplished this by revolutionary breakthrough concepts that liberate the planet for our use.

Population of the planet...

–150 Million in year 1...
–1 billion in 1804 (1803 years later)
–2 billion in 1927 (123 years later)
–3 billion in 1960 (33 years later)
–4 billion in 1974 (14 years later)
–5 billion in 1987 (13 years later)
–6 billion in 1999 (12 years later)

The fact that population has increased so dramatically and the corresponding fact that we have more of everything including food, leads to the conclusion that there are no limits. The illusion is that somewhere out there, just ahead of us is a limit to the resources of the planet and of the food supply and of the water supply. The premise is simple.... If we were nearing the end of our ability to survive on the planet as so many believe, then it would not be an event, but a process and we would be living less well each year with a lessening standard of living. Or, in retrospect, we would have died off long ago.

Here is a decision point in our considering our world view. We either see the earth as a ball of untapped resources, put here for our use, or we see it as a plot of limitations that we need to allow to govern our progress. That leads us to consider two age old philosophies that are characterized best by two differing schools of thought. The one is Pantheism – that we are from the earth and to be subject to it. The other is the Judeo-Christian view of reality in which the earth was created for mankind and given to us to use and master.

In one, our response is to stop the inventive use of the resources of the planet and to live with 'nature.' In the other we are free to explore, innovate and create. In fact it is our duty to fill up the earth and subdue it. The Judeo-Christian view of creation is that God made man, placed him over creation and

IF WE WERE NEARING THE END OF OUR ABILITY TO SURVIVE ON THE PLANET AS SO MANY BELIEVE, THEN IT WOULD NOT BE AN EVENT, BUT A PROCESS...

IF SO, WE WOULD HAVE DIED OFF LONG AGO!

released him to govern it with the command, "Fill the earth and subdue it." In that view of the planet and of creation, everything we need is here on or in the earth. So, the increase of population and of the use of the planet is not destructive but productive.

That does not mean that we have license to be destructive or to ignore the ecological systems that are present on the earth., What it does mean is that the limitations of energy, food sources and space is not determined by the earth itself but by the ingenuity of humanity. There is sufficient energy to power our future – it is simply a matter of finding and creating the sources. The energy used to this point did not evaporate from the planet into space somewhere. Energy simply changes forms it does not go away.

Everything we have used to this point of history was placed here in the beginning. So that same fact is constant. Everything we will need for the future is also already here. There is no lack and no shortage and no limits. The only point of restriction is in the mind of man and the ability to conceive of the need and the supply for the need. We hold the key to the future right inside the brain that God gave us.

On the one hand, the survival of the Pantheistic philosophies of reality would have us focus on our being subject to the earth and our limited view of its environments and resources. In this view, we are the victims of creation and of the earth and our best hope is that nature does not destroy us.

In opposition to this is the view of the earth as a garden plot that will yield answers to our needs if we but tend it and cultivate it. Here, in this basic tenant of our world view, we approach a wonderful revelation that has been hidden from view through much of human history. It is simply this: Creation, in its original formation, is not an end, but a beginning. God, who placed the earth in orbit and placed mankind on it, was not finished with all that He purposed. He was only starting the process of creation. He set the stage, placed the actors on the stage and then gave a command: Fill it up and subdue it. Everything that has happened from that point until now, is in fact, an ongoing work of creation. It is, if you will, the partnering of humanity with deity in bringing about the ultimate intention of God. We are instruments of ongoing creation, working, however unwittingly, the will of divine purpose.

There are no limits.

This is also true of money. Economics is not an exact science in the sense that economists disagree philosophically in their view. Some see a closed system of value in which one person having more than another is somehow wrong for they are thus taking their increased portion from others. If we shift our thinking to an open ended source of value and supply, then we conclude that there are no limits to the benefits, including financially, to the creation of value, products, services and the result of human ingenuity. This shift of economic world view is

19

a necessary step in being released from poverty and in becoming a player in the ongoing work of creation.

The communist/socialist philosophy of economics propose that the pie needs to be cut up evenly so that everyone gets a fair share. The free market philosophy of economics proposes quite the opposite – that we make our own pie and can create as many as we desire. Value is created and there is no limits to how much value can be created.

If there are no limits to what the earth can sustain, then it is also true that this same principle applies to every level of existence – including our personal lives. We have no limits. The only limits we have are those that we accept, those that we do not challenge and those that are self imposed.

Chapter Three

Secret # 2. Position is Everything

Our home sets on 74 acres of rural wonder. The views of the Sierra – Nevada range gives ample opportunity for admiration of the beauty of nature and a grateful heart for the privilege of being here. This year, my wife Linda decided to plant a garden. It has been several years since we have planted a garden, simply because it seems unnecessary with the ample supply of produce in the local supermarket. But, plant we did and before long the little plants began to sprout and find their way out of the ground. Then came the blooms. It seemed so miraculous, for without any conscious effort, the growth and blooms appeared, not because we struggled with them, but because we understood their nature and provided the ground and the water they needed to grow. Then came fruit – oh my, was there ever fruit. The tomatoes were abundant and oh so sweet, and the squash threatened to run us off. They were everywhere. There was enough for us, our friends, the local supermarket and possible a small town somewhere in a starving nation of the world.

And there was corn and watermelon and flowers galore. All we had to do was plant the seed. The harvest is in the seed, not in the struggle to get it to work. Have you ever watched people who seem to attract money and good things, while  others struggle hard with life and nothing happens for them? If we look carefully at each situation we will find several things…

It is not intelligence that releases resources.

I've met some really 'mentally challenged' people who seem to have a knack for making money. Everything they plant seems to come up green! And then there are those geniuses that can't seem to make a dime without someone else getting it away from them.

Years ago, when I was a young police officer I was in the rail yard, making a sweep. It was a common practice to move the vagrants along because there was always a constant problem in town along the rail line of petty theft, burglary, and other nuisance crimes. While doing one of these sweeps, I came upon a camp with several vagrants and one struck me as being different. He was articulate, reasonable and so we began to talk. He said he was a physician from back east who had left his practice and was now a homeless vagrant. He recounted a story of an unfaithful wife, a nasty divorce, the pressure of mounting bills, and of his decision to throw it all away and seek the freedom of traveling the rail lines. To affirm his story he reached into his pack and produced his diploma and is business license.

No, being smart or well educated does not, in and of itself, guarantee success in life. There is something more.

It is not extreme effort that releases resources.

While it is true that effort builds physical strength and that effort will affect obstacles in our life, simply working harder does not necessarily equate to success. There are some very unsuccessful people who work very hard at their skill or craft and seem to get further in the financial hole with each step. There are others who seem to be able to work but a few hours a day and make enormous amounts of money. It is not the amount of effort that makes the difference between success and failure.

And we could go on with an endless classification of attributes we admire in people that in and of their self does not make a difference in the degree of wealth that they attract.

Resource flow through the universe on a continuum much as does electricity. If you are in the right position, they flow to you. If you are not, they flow past you without including you in their context. Position is everything. That position is not a physical place or an educational level or a club that you can join. It is a position in the universe that you discover and that you assume. It is an attitude and a worldview that positions you to plug into the flow of wealth rather than fight for it.

Secret # 2 is that you can change your view of reality and with the change of position, plug into the stream of wealth that is present in our earth and flows freely to those who understand its nature. Wealth is not an accumulation of  resources by effort or by intelligence or by trickery. It is a position we assume that brings us to the flow points of wealth. Money flows to the wealthy, not because they deserve it or manipulate its flow, but because of their attitude and understanding of the universe.

I decided, after looking at the wealthy I knew, that money did not corrupt their thinking after it arrived. They thought differently about the world of wealth and resource before it arrived. Their thought process attracted wealth.

What really amazed me in looking at wealthy people was that they seemed to be less concerned about money than I was. While I was struggling to make a living, they were playing with resources as though it was some sort of game. Money was not their goal; it was the end result of their living within a different reality than I was living in.

The best illustration I find in the world around us is in the agricultural picture. The productivity is in the seed. The seed brings forth after its own kind. We do not have to struggle to release its productivity, just water and wait. What is necessary is to learn where to plant, and when to water. All of nature operates on the same principle. Most of the world is comprised of economic hunters and gatherers. We are nomadic in a sense, searching for where the money is and moving about to discover it. The key to value is not in finding it but in creating it. The key to wealth is not in getting the money, but in creating the value from the resources we each have within us and around us.

Wealth is found in a position not in a place. If you discover the mental position, it will flow to you.

Chapter 4

Secret # 3 – The Value is in the Thought

Everything starts with a thought. Inventions are not the end result of stacking junk randomly in a place and discovering that it ends up being something of value.  Inventiveness is the ability to think of something that is, in your thought, possible, then pursuing avenues of giving birth to it. Ben Franklin's experiments with electricity and Edison's experiments with harnessing it into a light bulb all started with a thought. Any accomplishment in human history did not start with a product or service and the subsequent discovery of how to use it, they all started with a thought of possibility and the creation of a process of discovery in putting that thought into reality.

While we have talked already about there being no limits, we also need to understand that nothing is impossible that we can conceive of. There is no shortage of energy, food supply or natural resources. The shortages we face are in creative thoughts on how to solve the perception of shortage that we assume. Investment dollars are setting out there waiting for the thought that is creative enough to turn into a profitable product or service. The world is waiting for the creative genius to think! Investment dollars are waiting for the thought!

Think of the great advancements in medical science. Most of them have come about in the past 20 years or so. Think, if you dare, about the pace of those accomplishments increasing over the next 20 years. We are on the verge of the most prolific period of time in the history of medical science. There are still challenges and diseases that we have not conquered. Aids ravages much of Africa and the world. Cancer is still a major fear for us all. Heart disease continues to top the list as the major cause of death. Family tragedies surround the pain and suffering of the human race where we have not yet found a cure. But one major shift has take place almost universally in the healthcare field – we now believe that we can find the cures.

We have a friend who is working on a cure for diabetes. He is one of the most brilliant scientists I know; yet I do not know if he will succeed. It is not that I do not trust him – I do. It is not that he is not bright enough – he is. It is that I do not know if he will succeed before someone else beats him to it. We are on a fast track in our world, of medical discovery that is amazing to say the least. We are on the verge of extending human life by decades and making the quality of that life worth living.

Energy is also a field of massive inventive investigation. From the internal combustion engine at the turn of the century, we are now looking at power sources for our transportation needs that are as broad as the human mind. Fuel cells, the conversion of solar power, electrical storage systems, you name it – we are working on it, and I have every confidence that these thoughts will generate alternative sources of energy that will release us from oil dependence. And when it does, it will also change the face of the globe economically. As I write, the oil rich nations have enjoyed a lengthy period of the flow of capital into their hands. And, by and large they have not invested it back into the social structures of their societies. Unfortunately, although some of them rattle the sabers of war and look for regional conquest, they are economically poised for disaster.

They are one thought and one invention away from insignificance.

Think for a moment about the rapid revolution of our electronic world. One generation ago, there were no computers, no iPods, no internet, no cell phones, no TiVo's, no VHS, VCR, HDTV, CD's or DVD. In one short generation, the world of electronic and of our daily lives has been revolutionized. It did not start with a wayward electron, wandering about space looking for something to do. It started with an accumulation of thoughts and inventive steps that extrapolated a revelation of something that we did not know before.

The most powerful thing in the universe is a thought. It is the fuel that inventiveness thrives on and the road to all things that benefit humankind. Nothing happens without the foreshadowing of the thought. Most people are searching for the money. They dream of being lucky – of winning the lottery or of their boat coming in. They collect contest entries and lucky bottle caps in the hope of changing their life. Given the odds of winning anything in life, that is all an illusion. What we should be pursuing is the thought that will bring us into the world market of value to others.

CHAPTER 5

Secret # 4 – Discovering Your Unique Place.

There are no two fingerprints exactly alike. What an amazing fact! No two people are exactly alike. Our fingerprints are different, our eyes patterns are different, and our DNA is different. Of the 6.5 billion people alive today, let alone the countless  people who have lived on this planet before this time, no two are alike.

Linda and I were married in 1960, and traveled on our honeymoon to the Sierras, where we would ultimately make our home, then over the pass to the San Francisco Bay area to visit some dear friends. We were excited to visit with them and they thought they should show us a new phenomenon in the Bay Area and took us to the Height-Ashberry district of town to see the people. We were quite amazed to see the vast numbers of counter culture people, each dressed in a style that they said expressed their individuality, but which, to my view made them all alike. This was the beginning of the Hippy movement that we now look back on in comical amusement.

Fads come and go and with them we reveal the insecurity of the human race as we adapt our context to reflect the fad. We all move toward being accepted by dressing alike, acting alike or thinking alike. Political organizations define for us what we believe by being a part of them. Churches tend to work on conforming us to a certain mold of acceptability. Schools define our course of education and behavior and measure our progress with grades. We are regimented toward conformity to a model, contexted by legal measures that restrict our activities and grow up reaching for the acceptance that sameness provides.

But our value to humanity is not found in how we are alike, but in our individual difference. Creativity, by its very nature is outside of the norm. Our value is often found in how we depart from the conformity of the historic context of thinking and in our ability to think differently, to challenge the assumptions of the past and to think in terms of some unique application of truth that has not been thought of yet.

Who was it that first looked at animal hair or plant fiber and conceived of weaving it into a thread and then extrapolated that the thread could be woven into a cloth and the cloth made into clothing? We look at our modern day retail clothing stores as though they have always been there, but realistically, there was a time when we wore animal skins and nothing more. Someone stopped to think beyond the group and to challenge the norm and to see something as an individual that had not been thought of yet.

Committees tend to remove individuality and reduce creativity to that which all members of the committee can agree upon. We agree upon what we know and understand. The new and different we tend to distrust and to fear. And yet it is in the new that progress is made. It is in the unique that we transcend the known and move into the arena of revelation that is the building block of human invention. Be very careful that you do not allow your creative genius to be dampened by the norm and the need for acceptance. Acceptance is often found in conformity. Creative genius is often misunderstood by the committee. It is wise to listen to your critics, but if you only move forward when everyone thinks you are sane, you will forever be caught in the matrix of working harder at the same thing and contributing nothing unique to the world.

Who was it that watched the pot boil and realized that the force that lifted the pot lid would lift anything else? It was this unique questioning and thinking that gave rise to the steam engine and later to the internal combustion engine.

Who was it that watched the tree roll down the hill and thought of making slices of the log and putting an axle between them and thus invented the wheel?

Without order, nothing can move and work. Without chaos, nothing can evolve. In this context, chaos is the result of something not fitting into the conformed structure. That is, there has to be the individuality of discovery for inventiveness to result. Then, there has to be the application of that inventiveness to the existing structures around it for it to have any intrinsic value to the world it is presented to.

Being unique and individualistic is essential, but then it has to seek value and application to the world that is waiting for it. Revelation in isolation is valueless. Revelation and the sale of the thought and the idea is the essential next step. While one has to be an individual to explore and find their value, one cannot be a rebel on top of it and expect to benefit from the revelation of creativity.

CHAPTER 6

Secret # 5. There is NO They

I was very fortunate to have grown up in an intact home with traditional role models and very little worries. We were not rich by any economic standards, but Dad was hard working and our basic needs were met. By any other standard other than economic standards, we were rich. We ate together, played together, vacationed together and spent our evenings around the piano singing harmony to familiar hymns.

Dad was a strong personality and set a loving boundary of protection around the family. I never questioned whether or not we would have something to eat or if Santa would arrive for Christmas or if the world would treat me fairly. Dad would take care of it. I never wondered if Dad would come home drunk – he did not drink. I never wondered if I would get beaten in a fit of rage. Dad would always be fair. Mom would always be there when I got up, getting us ready for school and packing our lunch. She would always be there when I got off the bus and would take care of our clothing, the housework and the domestic chores. They always took care of it.

Then something happened. I grew to the point that I could manage putting my own clothes in the washer, packing my own lunch and doing my own chores. Soon, I had to feed the dog, the rabbits and the chickens. I also got a part of the yard that was mine to weed and other responsibilities that I would take care of. They would not do it for me any longer.

Then I got a job, started paying rent for my room and utilities and increasingly 'they' did not take care of those things for me any longer. I was on a track of self-sufficiency that would lead to getting married and moving into my own fatherly roll. Many years later I lost my Dad and a couple of years later, my Mom. I was privileged to officiate at both of their funerals and to understand that they had done it right. They made sure that I was taken care of as long as I could not take care of myself, but increasingly they reinforced the self-sustaining attributes that led me to take care of myself. They are gone now: There is no 'they.'

What I also was conditioned to accept is that in the world of complex problems and changing social structures: There is no they!

History is filled with the stories of human bondage. To some degree, humanity must love bondage, for we have permitted so much of it. It is not just the dictator with the biggest gun; it is the politician in any form of government who promises to take care of us. They seem to surface as the winner of the political process.

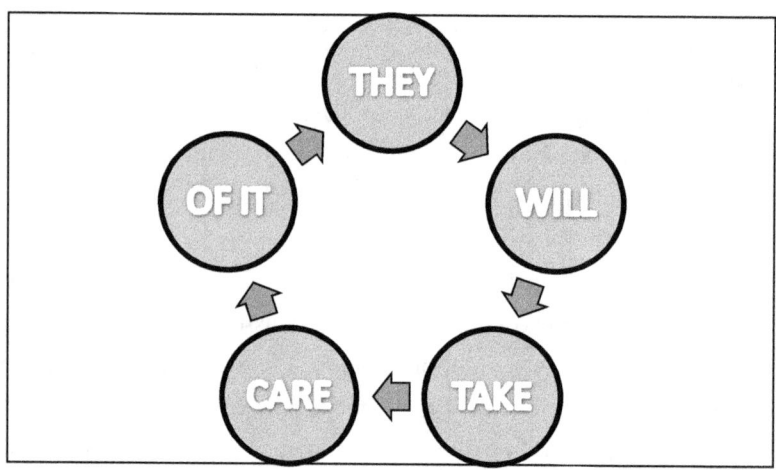

Problem: THERE IS NO THEY!

We are conditioned to think that those who lead us are wise enough and connected enough and powerful enough to take care of the evils that threaten us. THEY can do it! They have knowledge that we do not have and resources we do not understand and they can ultimately fix anything. THEY will take care of us.

One of the secrets that we have to understand is that there is no boat to come in, you will probably not hit the lottery, no one is going to knock on your door with a huge check for 10 million dollars, and Bill Gates is not going to put you in his will. Neither chance nor the illusive THEY are going to do for you what you must do for yourself.

There is something very healthy about identifying that illusion in our thinking and rejecting it. It frees us to take the action to make for ourselves what others are not going to make for us. It certainly must be a secret for the average person in our world is waiting for their luck to change, wanting for the government program to kick in, waiting for their numbers to come up, waiting for someone to throw the change of chance in their direction.

One of the greatest financial revelations one will ever have is to realize that – THERE IS NO THEY! You are it! What you create is all there will be for you. Scary thought? It need not be, for just as we considered the planet on which we live and the infinite resources it contains for us and the conclusion that "There is No Limit," that same conclusion can be made for you.... Inside of you are the thoughts, the possibilities and the energy to take care of yourself and to produce an abundance of whatever you need. You are a miraculous organism, endued by your creator with not only the rights we see enumerated in the Bill of Rights, but also with the potential to accomplish great things within the strengths that you possess.

What is the potential of the human personality? What can a person accomplish? Why is it that some people accomplish so much and some so little? Is it that some people have all the luck? Is it that God looks down from His heavenly seat and determines to give one person all the money, brains and good fortune, while looking at you and decides He just doesn't like you much?

No, if we look at those questions critically, we have to conclude that we are all different but that does not mean that some have greater value or potential. It simply means that in the infinite variety of human difference, our potential is not found in our sameness or in our ability to do what others can do, but is found in our uniqueness. To reach ones full potential, we have to capitalize on our difference and market that uniqueness. Your difference and the skill that it affords you is your ticket to greatness in life.

That uniqueness plus your rejection of the existence of the THEY, will set you free to reach beyond the norm and rise to your highest place in life. Remember: God Doesn't Make Junk!

One of the great differences between those who accumulate wealth and those who don't is this simple fact: Those who have wealth do not depend on others to get it for them nor do they wait for chance to bring it. They create it. They assume that they have the ability and the wisdom to make it without the THEY - and then they do.

CHAPTER 7

Secret # 6 – It's OK to be Wrong!

Oh my gosh! What a terrible thing to propose, especially when most of the world is fighting to be right. Somewhere in the underpinnings of our human frame is the illusion that being right is the highest thing we can be in life. Religions argue that they are right because they have a better, or more right, interpretation of scriptures. They labor to contrast and compare their message and understanding with those of other religions and always come to the same wonderful conclusion: We are right.

Politics is underpinned by the same set of contrasts and conclusions. Economists disagree, scientists disagree and every profession, philosophy, religion and neighbor concludes by contrast that they are more right than the person they are analyzing. There is something wonderful about being right, but it requires that everyone else must by contract, be wrong. There are those who want to kill us because they are right and we are wrong. To us it seems absurd, but to those who ascribe to this obsession with being right, it makes perfect sense.

There is bondage in this continuum that is dangerous and which, if allowed to rule ones focus in life, will stop progress. There is security in being right, but if security is found only in the arrangement of facts in our brain in a certain order or sequence so that we are right, then to change means that I have to be willing to admit that I am wrong. If we are only secured by our rightness, then we are apt to continue through life with the same ideas, the same level of adventure and the same thoughts, simply run over and over in our mind.

But to do so is the definition of insanity. Sure, we have all heard the little saying: Insanity is doing the same thing over and over and expecting a different result. But isn't that the most common pattern of living for most people? Convinced that they are right, they do the same thing, drive the same route, talk to the same people, listen to the same program and hope that somewhere in the dull and bland routine of rightness, some stroke of luck will lift them out of the pattern of action and result and there will be a fortune arrive at their door.

But it doesn't happen that way does it. Isn't it better to assume that the reason I am getting the results I am getting is because of the process I am following and if I want more or something different, I will have to alter my mind set and my actions to release that different result. In other words, I have to admit that I do not yet know everything I should know in order to get what I want. Put another way, I am wrong at least part of the time, I just do not know where. That is the nature of secrets. They are not just an expansion of the knowledge I have or of the information available through my current set of friends and acquaintances. The secret is, they are wrong also. What we are talking about is not just an adjustment of our known facts or a rearrangement of our data. What we are talking about is what Abraham Maslow called a "peak experience." It is one of those kinds of experiences in which we have a total paradigm shift and our worldview is altered.

So far, in these chapters we have discussed many items of illusion in our common beliefs. The attempt has been to alter ones perception of reality. That comes by an openness to be willing to journey into those changing possibilities and the acknowledgement that I do not yet know it all. In this is the abandonment of the need to be secure in a pat set of facts and positions (being right) and a willingness to acknowledge that I

36

may not be right in all things but I am willing to explore other things.

I stood in front of the graduating class of the college that I had helped to start in Southern California. I was speaking to the first graduating class of the Bible College that is now over 40 years old. I told them that I had a confession to make, that probably half of what I had taught them was wrong. I just didn't know which half. It was their job to take what they had learned and test it against the experiences of their world and find what was real and what was the accumulation of data that

"Half of what I taught you is wrong. Problem is: I don't know which half."

simply did not work. They laughed, but I was dead serious. We are all, to some degree or another, dead wrong. The problem is, we do not know it. In our search to be secure and significant it never occurs to us that an attitude of challenging what we think to be real is far more productive than resting on the assumption of being right.

Seek then to be wrong – that is seek to uncover those bastions of knowledge that we all have that are incomplete, inconsistent, unproductive, unloving, unkind and unfruitful in our lives. They are hindrances to getting what we really want and what our destiny allows us to reach for. It has been said that the average person only uses 5% of their mind and only achieves 10% of their potential. If that is anywhere near true, we have so much more to learn and so much more to believe for. Life is designed to be a banquet of goodness and most of the world is starving to death.

Learning should be a lifelong challenge never a plateau that we arrive at. Sometime I wonder if achieving a degree is a good thing in that some have the illusion that they have by that measured landmark, arrived where they should be. Life is not designed to be an arrival but a journey. To make the most of it, we are obligated to continue the learning and changing process throughout the course of our journey. Without that adventure of vulnerability to our stature of rightness, we will stop at some secure point or perspective and assume that we have arrived. When we do, life is over. We are right, but we are no longer real.

The great secret of growth and the revolution of our understanding is that the goal is never to be right but to be real! That is a great secret that is hidden from most of our world.

If we do not change our direction, we are liable to end up where we are headed.

It doesn't matter how long you have been going down the wrong road, turn around! Now!

"It is not what we don't know that gets us into trouble, it is what we absolutely know for sure – that isn't so." Yogi Berra

CHAPTER 8

Secret #7 The Structure is Wealth

Statically, the average American spends 115% of what they earn each year. This is a simple formula discovered by averaging into the national income averages, the increase of private debt figures. We are a society that is obsessed with instant gratification and our financial institutions have found new and creative ways of accommodating that obsession. Want a new house? You can get one with a 125% mortgage, leaving enough to furnish the house, pay off a few bills and have a good time. What they may not emphasize is that in 3 years the interest rate will go up to the usual rate for such a loan and your payment will increase to the point that you cannot pay for it.

The illusion of a good economy is a dangerous thing. The illusion that you can get more now and pay less for it in the long run is simply not mathematically possible. The old proverb is true, "The borrower is the slave of the lender." Bondage comes in many forms but this one is so easy to get into and so difficult to get out of.

The handling of wealth is a great responsibility. This past week the news told of a famous entertainer who was making over $700,000.00 per month and had no investments and no savings. The stories of those who allow money to slip through their fingers are legend. From sports figures, entertainers, authors, lottery winners to all of us. It doesn't matter how much money you make, if you do not provide the structure for keeping enough of it to use as a foundation for your life.

We have a friend who is wealthy in many ways, including financially. She worked at two jobs for enough years to get a retirement income from them. She lived simply through those years and saved her money, investing it in secure investments that over time increased her financial position. Now in retirement she has several streams of income, investments that are worth enough to allow her to travel, play and enjoy life.

I am not of the mindset that one should live so Spartan as to not be able to enjoy life, so I am not suggesting that living within the confines of a small income is the way that life should be lived. I usually opt to direct people to increase their income and increase the creativity that will get them there. But there is a simple principle to the accumulation of wealth that is larger than the amount of income. It is simply this: You have to spend less than you make.

This is the structure that will allow you to use the money that comes through you and to average out income over the good years, bad years and retirement years. If you are spending 115% of your income each year, the accumulated debt will tie you to the grindstone of routinely trying to keep up and pay the interest to someone else who has the foresight to spend less each year than they make and lend the rest to you. The lender, investor and the one with excess income over expenses are in the position to rule over those who do not have this simple discipline.

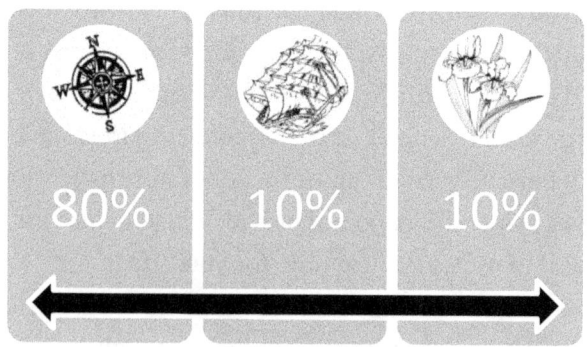

When I do a budget session with people I always try to lead them to the 80-10-10 budget. That is, regardless of what you make, learn to live on 80% of it or increase your income so that you can. Then save and invest 10%. You will be surprised to find out what will happen with this small portion over time given compound interest. It will become a lot of money. The other 10%, I believe should be given away – carefully. By that I mean that you should never give money to people who, although seeming unfortunate, will waste it or destroy themselves with it. Never support failure. I do feel sorry for those who stand on the street corner or freeway off ramp and beg, but I am also aware that giving to some people does not help them; it perpetuates the error of their condition and grounds them to failure.

The alternative is to invest in people who are headed for success or agencies that provide support to people who are making life-changing shifts toward self-sufficiency. Local churches, social agencies or children's programs are always a good investment. Not only is giving back to our community a good thing for the community, it is good for us to sow the seeds of success to others, for in that simple act of giving we release the harvest of blessing to ourselves.

For many, the practice of tithing provides an outlet for giving of 10% to their local church or a ministry that they are familiar with. This can advance one's own sense of purpose beyond what they can do as an individual and support purposes that are worthy of that support.

The principle is simple: Structure your spending so that you spend less than you make. With what is left over, pay yourself first. Invest in your future, and then help others. But in doing so always support success – never support failure.

The best investment you can make in yourself is to provide for the creative ideas you have. Education is a good way to develop our creative potential, but that creative investment can take many forms. It may be as simple as buying the tools or materials needed to try an invention or to secure the time to write a book, or to set at your piano and compose a new song. The possibilities are endless, but most people let the creative thoughts go by as they go through life without ever trying or stopping long enough to structure their thoughts into some creative application.

You not only owe it to yourself to explore your potential, you owe it to the world. What the world will become in the next century is being determined now, by you.

CHAPTER 9

Secret # 7 – Less is more

The modern American executive spends more than 55 hours a week at work and some work 7 days a week; taking work home, just to get ahead. The assumption of our culture is that the more we work, the more we will produce and with that increase in production, we will get closer to our goals, both personal and financial.

Here's the secret…. – It doesn't work that way.

Years ago I was introduced to a way of thinking that forever changed my life. It is called the Pareto Principle. It has been called the principle of factor divergence. Simply stated it means that, for most events, 80% of the effects comes from 20% of the causes. It is true in much of life. 20% of the people hold 80% of the wealth. 80% of the effect of our work is accomplished by 20% of our effort. 20% of the people create the companies that employee 80% of the population.

It is easy to step into any office and see this principle at work. If there are 100 people employed in the office, it is likely that 80 are busy doing the simple tasks that are created by the 20% who are the key figures in the organization. Those producers are not necessarily the owner or the manager, but you will spot them in a few minutes. Their influence and persona fill the entire building.

If this is true in general in the economic and work world, then it is also true in our daily lives. As I look at my desk, I see the Pareto Principle in full view. There are stacks of papers that need attention, but there are only a few that will really matter if they get attention or not. It is the 20% of the tasks that will accomplish 80% of the goals and the rest, in the last analysis do not matter much. They are important to somebody, but they do not have to be important to me.

We have all learned to make lists of activities that we are committed to but often we do not structure those 'to-do' lists with this principle in mind. We just start the day doing those which give us the most pressure. The secret to success is to daily structure those items so that those with the greatest importance are the first that we tackle and that we do not quit moving through the list until the items we start are finished. By the end of the day, we will have made major movement toward our goals, and those things that are most pressing will just fade away on their own.

The tendency is for the average human being to tackle the most urgent first and to prioritize the easiest items first. That way, they will be busy keeping those who send them the pressure at bay while justifying their time on the job. While that approach may fill in the time and make people think you are getting things done, those things in the last analysis, may have little importance to the overall objectives of the job and the company.

Being busy and spending time is not the goal. Let's hear that again! Business and the passing of time is not our objective and can be counterproductive.

Sometimes, ignoring the press of the urgent is essential to moving in a straight line toward the goal. Here are some ways that have helped me over the years to get done what I wanted to do...

Start by stopping long enough to think.

The idea is the goal. Without a clear picture of the idea and the goal that it presents, activity is wasted.

Some years ago a safety inspector came to me to tell me that the ladder some workers were using was unsafe. I accompanied him to the site and assured him that he was absolutely right. The problem was, the ladder was not leaning against our building, it was on the building next door. That represents the mind set of much of the world we live in. We can become so focused on the condition of the ladder that we fail to ask if it is leaning on the right building.

Movement without a vision builds ruts. The letter of the law kills, the scriptures tell us, but the spirit of the law focuses it on what is intended. Did you ever meet a officer of the law who was officious? They are not usual, but when you meet one you cringe knowing this mindless human law book is missing the point of what the law intended.

That's right…. It is important to start by stopping. Stop and think. Stop and plan. Stop and crystallize the vision of who you are and where you are going. Otherwise all the activity in the world will not make up for the scattered aimlessness that results.

Write the vision.

If you cannot articulate it, you do not yet have it focused. Write it, rewrite it and go over it again, until that inner voice lets you know it is complete, ready and it has inspired fire in your soul. Nothing great is accomplished without the enthusiasm that comes from knowing exactly what you are after.

Document it in such a way that the enthusiasm you feel for it is catching and others are excited about it.

Make it unique.

If you plan to start a nationwide hamburger franchise chain, you might consider not using the name McDonald's. First of all, you will get sued if they find out. Secondly, they have already captured an image and a reputation that is daunting. If you are going to compete for their market, you better have something different enough to inspire the customer to come to you.

Your difference is your value. Creating what already exists is not creating at all. Who would have thought that Starbucks would have ruined the slogan for beggars around the world – "Hay mister, do you have a nickel for a cup of coffee?" No self respecting beggar can justify saying, "Hay mister, do you have $15.00 for a moco-frappy-fuzzy-thingy and a muffin?" Yet this unique chain has grown phenomenally by doing something that no one else ever dreamed possible.

What is your gifting? What do you love to do? What kind of people do you love to be around, doing what? Sometimes it is your hobby that is the guide to your future.

Get started.

The usual mind set is that I will start when I have the money to afford it. But that is backwards. Money is attracted to great ideas, not the other way around. If you start acting like money is not the problem, the great idea will move you into the stream of money that you need. There is never a money problem, only an idea problem.

Break the vision into sequential steps and then start with the first one and do nothing else until it is finished. When it is finished, go on to the next step.... But be prepared, reality is often different than the idea in your head. Be prepared to refine the goal and the tasks, and reorganize the steps, but do not ever lose sight of the vision itself.

Keep the focus on the high priorities.

While moving down the path toward you idea, be sure to prioritize the activities you engage in. Delegate as much of the lower level tasks as you can and do the important things first. The end result will be that you discover the secret of the Pareto

Principle – 20% of your effort will produce 80% of your results and the rest will hardly matter. Rather than trying to do everything, let some of them go... Go fishing, talk to your kids, take your dog for a walk and take a weekend to be

Less is More

at home with those you love. The rest will become meaningless in time. You do not have to do it all.

Less is more.... That's just the way life is. Plug into it and watch it revolutionize your life and your time. Time is the difference.... Everyone is given the same amount of it each day, but some serve time while others make time serve them. The difference is a secret to be understood and a choice to make.

Chapter 10

Secret # 8 – There is no fair share.

I used to love to dish out the ice cream at home for my sisters and myself; in that I could give the three of them equal shares and take an extra share for myself. But Mom got wise to my manipulations and decided that whoever dished out the desserts had to let the others take first choice of the dish and the server got last choice. From then on, all of the portions were equal.

Equality is a difficult concept in our world, and we tend to have mixed feelings about it, and receive mixed messages about what is equal and what is fair. Whole social and economic systems are spawned based on how a culture feels about what is one's fair  share and what we are entitled to. The basis of socialism and communism is the belief that there is only so much to go around and that if one person gets more than their share, then someone else is deprived of their fair share.

We are conditioned from childhood to think in these terms. Everyone is created equal and deserves their fair share, we are told. But experience tells us that not everyone is equal on the playground and life is not ultimately fair. There are those who have superior athletic ability and they are always chosen first for the team while others wait until last because no team captain really wants them on their team. And it continues through life. Some people have great skill while others seem inept. Genetics are not equal and neither is the distribution of values.

By the time we have graduated from college, we have learned to compensate for our weaknesses and capitalize on our strengths. If athletics is not in our skill set, we are probably spending our time doing more rewarding tasks. If we are not a super model in physical appearance, we have probably come to grips with it and are set in some other line of work. Experience over time provides us with a definition of who we are and what we can and cannot do and sets for us an identity and our expectations of life.

Although we would all affirm that we are created equal in value, I doubt that anyone would argue that we are all created the same in personality, ability, perspective, appearance, body type, mental abilities or station in life. The concept of equality has been sold as some cookie cutter sameness that we should aspire to. But it is not the order of nature or the end result of any social experiment in history. Some are smarter. Some are more attractive. Some have that unique ability to see opportunity when it arrives, while others would not recognize it if it were to run over them.

The premise of equality in value as a measure of respect and honor is certainly a worthy goal, but beyond that, there is no way to guarantee a fair share of life's resources. In fact the pursuit of an evenhanded distribution of wealth is an illusion. Wealth is not a pie to be cut up and given out equally. It is a reflection of what we create and provide that others are willing to pay for, thus by its very nature wealth is unequal.

Now get ready, because I am going to tell you that this is not only the way it is intended to be, it is good that it is this way. Personal motivation for an increase in our world is a good thing. It drives us to produce, to excel and to create. Economic systems that are tyrannical or are aimed at equality in distribution, reduce personal motivation and always fail. If I am guaranteed the same as anyone else, why try to excel? Why try to do more, be more or grow? Communism fell, not because we went to war against it, but because the seed of failure were in the system.

The secret is that money flows to value. The interesting thing about people of wealth is that they seldom seek money as a thing in itself. Money is only a means of measuring success. Their motivation is not to gain the money but to win the game of capital enterprise. They are usually risk takers, game players and entrepreneurs, set to explore the values of the world they have created and to win at the competitive edge of the game of life.

Shortly after our moving to Reno, many years ago now, a mutual friend introduced me to a local inventor named Bill Lear. Bill was a fascinating fellow who would spend days without sleep working incessantly on his next invention. He allowed for no diversion from his focused task of figuring out a way to create the thing that was only a thought in his head. Bill created more than 150 patents, but did not seem to care much about his past accomplishments or his accumulation of wealth. He was simply driven to keep inventing.

The path to wealth is in the creation of value. Value has no limit and has no definition. It is that which we create that others are willing to pay for and/or use. It can be a product, goods, services, or simply an idea that people will follow. There are endless stories of those who have pursued value and have subsequently blessed the human race. And there are yet remaining, an endless stream of value ideas, waiting to be thought, to be defined and to be produced. There is no end to the production of value.

Just over 100 years ago:

- Consider that, 4,000 years ago few of the items we use daily existed.

- Most of the major companies we look to today as the icons of valued production did not exist 100 years ago.
- The average life expectancy was 47 years.
- Only 14 percent of the homes had a bathtub.
- Only 8 percent of the homes had a telephone.
- There were only 8,000 cars and only 144 miles of paved roads.
- The maximum speed limit in most cities was 10 mph.
- The tallest structure in the world was the Eiffel Tower!
- The average wage in 1907 was 22 cents per hour.
- The average worker made between $200 and $400 per year .
- A competent accountant could expect to earn $2000 per year, a dentist $2,500 per year, a veterinarian between $1,500 and $4,000 per year, and a mechanical engineer about $5,000 per year.
- More than 95 percent of all births took place at HOME .
- Ninety percent of all doctors had NO COLLEGE EDUCATION! Instead, they attended so-called medical schools, many of which were condemned in the press AND the government as 'substandard.'
- Sugar cost four cents a pound.
- Eggs were fourteen cents a dozen.
- Coffee was fifteen cents a pound.
- Most women only washed their hair once a month, and used Borax or egg yolks for shampoo.

- Canada passed a law that prohibited poor people from entering into their country for any reason.
- Five leading causes of death were:
  1. Pneumonia and influenza
  2. Tuberculosis
  3. Diarrhea
  4. Heart disease
  5. Stroke
- The American flag had 45 stars.
- The population of Las Vegas, Nevada, was only 30!!!!
- Crossword puzzles, canned beer, and ice tea hadn't been invented yet.
- There was no Mother's Day or Father's Day.
- Two out of every 10 adults couldn't read or write.
- Only 6 percent of all Americans had graduated from high school.
- Marijuana, heroin, and morphine were all available over the counter at the local corner drugstores. Back then pharmacists said, 'Heroin clears the complexion, gives buoyancy to the mind, regulates the stomach and bowels, and is, in fact, a perfect guardian of health.' (Shocking? DUH!)
- Eighteen percent of households had at least one full-time servant or domestic help.
- There were about 230 reported murders in the ENTIRE ! U.S.A. !

The future is bright and the value elements of the future are waiting for those who will dream, apply and pursue their being understood and implemented. There are no limits to value.

So what is a fair share? What is fair changes year by year in the economic world? What is ultimately fair is to be determined by the one having the value to share and the one wanting to purchase it. The end result will always be an exchange that is agreeable to both, good for both but will leave someone having more wealth than others. This is not evil – this is progress.

Chapter 11

Secret # 9 – Wealth has an emotional basis.

We are told that $2 + 2 = 4$, as though that is all there is to the hard cold facts of mathematics and economics. But the reality is, $2 + 2$ in a negative emotional context can become "0" in no time, while 2 by itself in a positive context can become 10,000. Some economists have proposed this emotional context theory for what is happening economically for a long time, while others try to ignore anything other than the hard cold rules of math.

The crash of the 20's was precipitated by bad news and a run on the banks, depleting reserves and stopping any further business. What would have happened if no one had listened to the news and no one had tried to save himself or herself from the predicted disaster? The economy does rise and fall based on how we feel about it. That is true individually and it is also true collectively. If we feel negative about our financial future we will tend to pull in, close down and seek security over progress. The same with a national economy. If we hear enough bad news we will do the same. In fact, I believe that the chief affect agent in an economy is not the numbers, the production capacity, the capital investment or other economic factors; it is the emotion and the outlook. A positive economic outlook generates expansion while a negative outlook generates contraction.

Productivity for an individual or a nation is also heavily influenced by the emotion and outlook of the future. We feel energized to act and to grow when we believe that good things are awaiting our effort. Conversely, if our efforts are not going to be rewarded, or if we feel they are not, we tend to reduce the energy focused into the task. Energy flows to that which is increasing.

We all walk the fine line between success and failure, and there are times when we are uncertain as to which side of the line we are on. What keeps us on one side of that line or the other is often our attitude. If we believe we are going to succeed, then we attract positive people and positive situations into our lives and into the process of life. If however we are given to a depressive attitude we will tend to attract people and situations that are compatible with the atmosphere we create. Like attracts like. We create the atmosphere and it attracts the end result.

I have a good friend who always seemed to be successful at everything he touched. I finally decided that I would make a study of his methods of doing business to see if I could figure out what he was doing and why it was always successful. I looked for a financial formula, but there did not seem to be one. I looked for a management style, but this guy was sometimes organized and sometimes scattered. I looked for some key to what he was doing and the results he was getting. I even went to work with him one day to see the details of what he did, but there was no pattern that I could identify that would account for the results that he obtained. Finally, one day it hit me. It was none of the things I had looked for, it was simply his attitude. He believed that what he was doing was the greatest thing going on in the world at the time. It was contagious. Everyone he touched either joined with him in making the project a success or they ran from him. Either way, he won.

The atmosphere determines the result. The attitude determines the atmosphere. I've read a lot of books on success and frankly, I found most of them without substance, but all have one simple item high on their presentation agenda – what you think about determines your future. I read one recently that said little if anything except that what you think about you attract. It is not as simple as that, but it is as important as that. Disciplined thinking sets expectation, goals, and focuses our energy. It becomes a context that filters out negative and counterproductive people and activities. It generates energy toward activities that create a process toward those goals and becomes the stairway that leads to success. Activity is necessary, but it is effortless when it is energized and motivated.

I have met a few people who are set on a path of persistent negativity. Everything is bad and there is nothing you can do to talk them out of it. They appeal to their sense of reality and refuse to accept the notion that reality is created. For them reality is reality and there is nothing one can do about it. But let me argue that reality is interpretive and it is not permanent. Reality changes. Times change. The world is changing moment by moment as we go through time and space. Nothing is set in stone, so to speak. What reality will become tomorrow can be left to fate and chance or it can be determined, created and altered by our actions and attitude. Attitude therefore, IS reality.

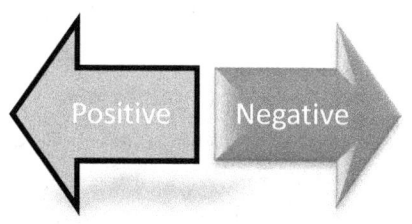

Our future is more determined by emotion, energy, attitude and the atmosphere we create than it is by some blind happenstance of fate. The greatest thing you can do for your future is to determine to think positive and productive thoughts, create a positive context and let that atmosphere focus your activities into successful endeavors. The focused move aggressively toward their goals and they arrive. The passive are ambivalent and afraid and allow the supposed failure that they fear to overtake them without a fight.

There will always be a difference in our economic stature in this world. Some will always attract wealth and some will always be poor. If you ask 100 poor people why it is that the good life has passed them by, they will give 100 different excuses for their fate. It will be the fault of other people, of circumstances beyond their control or of the government who refused to put them in a program. And, if you ask 100 successful people how they got there, you will hear them all tell different stories of how their plans brought them to where they are. The poor will tend to blame while the successful will tend to tell of their responsibility.

Blame is the emotional discharge for failure. It is the excuse for one's personal plight. Never allow blame to be part of your emotions. We can't always control other people or circumstances, but the issue is not the events of our history but what we do with them. Life is not a single event; it is the accumulation of small steps and a series of events leading to a life style. The greatest influence in our lives is not the seriousness of the events but the emotion that we choose in response to them. That's right, success or failure is not a destiny, it is a choice we make as to how to conduct the journey. The end result will take care of itself.

The atmosphere we are in is created, therefore it can be changed. The objective is to live each day in the present, making it as beautiful as we can, while planning for the future – for that is where we will spend the rest of our life. If you believe that your life is worth living, your belief will create that reality. If you give love and joy into your life, life will give back to you that same love and joy. We reap what we sow. This is an

57

unalterable fact of life. The world is like a mirror, reflecting back to you what you display in it.

Success or failure, joy or pain, love or hate, courage or fear, all are choices we make not the results of blind fate.

Chapter 12

Secret #10 – Nice Guys Finish First

I have several heroes left over from my childhood. Evenings beside the radio, listening to the adventures of the super heroes of the day left me with an indelible impression of good and evil, right and wrong, and of the sterling character of those who led the fight for justice. My Dad and my Uncle seemed to fit that role. Dad was a country preacher who genuinely loved people and his role in their lives. My Uncle Ralph was a California Highway Patrol Officer and in charge of Motorcycle Training in Los Angeles. I followed in both of their footsteps, becoming a police officer at the ripe old age of 22, while continuing my education to become a minister.

Police Academy was quite a shock for me. I had signed up to help people and to protect my community. You know – The Lone Ranger of Colton, California. The Lone Ranger never hurt anyone but always won the day. He could shoot the gun out of the bad guys hand at 400 yards from the hip. No one ever died on that program and everyone lived happily ever after as the bad 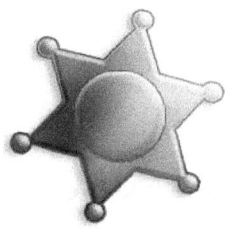 guy went to prison and the Lone Ranger rode off into the sunset – "Hi Ho Silver, Away!" But the academy told me that bad guys do not give you the opportunity for aim for the hand and you have to shoot to stop them – center mass! Shoot to kill? What kind of hero was I to be?

It was not long into my street experience that I encountered the reality of human cruelty. There really were evil people out there who were bent on cruel deeds. Being raised in a pastor's home we had been prepared for the finer points of sin. We knew to avoid evil thoughts, not saying please and thank you and we were also trained to avoid close association with kids who used bad language and did not shower regularly. That was the context of evil in my childhood. But I was now thrust into the middle of dark streets, pimps, prostitutes, robbers, thieves, child abusers and murderers. There was a level of human depravity I had never experienced and did not want to acknowledge. I knew there was  "so much bad in the best of us and so much good in the worst of us, that it hardly behooved any of us to talk about the rest of us!" But my experience did not fit with the clichés of childhood. There were some people who were genuinely evil and who, on occasion, put themselves in a position that needed police confrontation. Sometimes you have to shoot people!

I suppose I was always known as a nice guy and tried hard to have good relationships with everyone, but I was in a position that I had to either modify my attitude and understanding of life or change careers. One fellow, in one instant of time did that for me. He had stolen a semi-truck and trailer and when I came across his path and tried to stop him, he decided to not stop. The truck was not fast enough to out run me and finally got hung up on a telephone pole as he tried to make a turn. I ran to the driver's door and ordered him out and one the ground, but her refused, so I reached up and pulled him down... He came down – right on top of me, spun me around, got me in a choke hold and had his hand on my gun. It is difficult to explain what goes on in the human mind at a time like that, but in an instant my entire life was review mentally and the concluding thought was, "he's going to kill you and he will not take care of your wife and children." My training took over and I got out of the hold, spun around on him and had him down and cuffed in one simple motion. I amazed myself, but more, I realized that I was going to kill him if need be – and without hesitation.

Nice guys finish last, we are told, and in the grim streets of human depravity, this is true. The need to survive produces strange and wonderful emotions and actions that move us toward human survival. But within the arena of our day-to-day affairs of life, we never want to become them. "Them" are the ones for whom laws are made. It is because of "Them" that police exist and weapons of self-preservation are fashioned. They consume our time and resources, but the most important thing about "Them" is to not become one of them!

Periodically, in the conflict between law and disorder, cynicism tells us that they do not deserve a fair trial, that they are unworthy of justice and proper procedures, but any movement out of our proper place of authority and we are in danger, for we are at that moment operating at their level and by their rules and we are – Them! The thin blue line of law enforcement is an essential part of social order, but it must always operate on a different level and with higher purpose than the element that we exist to deter. It is never OK to become "Them."

Somewhere at the core of the human frame is a love shaped hole that can be fulfilled by nothing other than the love it was designed to contain. It is that love factor that completes us as human beings and makes our lives full and healthy. It is the loss of that quality that creates evil and gives place to the cruelty of human depravity. Someone once asked me how I could wrestle another human being to the ground, put handcuffs on them and take them to jail? My response was easy and instant, "Easy," I replied; "I am not doing anything to them. They have done it to themselves. I am simply the messenger of justice, helping them learn to face their responsibility to themselves and others. I am blessing them by getting help for them and seeing that they do not injure themselves or others in the process of growing up and learning to live right." It is not an equal opposite role; it is a role of coming along side to help, even without their invitation at times. It need not be of equal cruelty even where force is necessary. It can be an act of love for the person gone wild.

We must find that core belief in the love of God for us and of our extending that core value to the world around us. Love does, in fact, make the world go around. Love need not be weak, without character, permissive or without definition. In fact, love must be strong, definitive, giving, and willing to do the tough stuff when necessary. Love is after the good end result, not the easy road to it.

So you see, I do believe that good wins and evil looses. Although the Lone Ranger was unrealistic in his pursuit of non-violence, he was a hero none-the-less. There is a terrible tendency in our culture that says that strength wins or that the more powerful get the best, or that the accumulation of power is what life is about. We see it in athletics, politics and business. If we are not careful, we abandon time honored principles of right and wrong to seek advantage and power. We take short cuts to success and find ways of climbing over the bodies of our victims to get to the top. But the end result is, we have become "Them" and whatever it is that we get, is an empty bag of waste, not fit to be a worthy prize for our efforts.

It may appear at times that the cruel win or that the unprincipled get the advantage, but it is never ultimately the case. In the end, given enough time, evil will show its colors and the nice people, who are committed to love of life, love of others and love of self will be found at the top. The problem may be in defining where the top is!

Nice guys do finish first!

Chapter 13

Secret # 11 – Success is Never Final

I walked into his office on the 10th floor of the high-rise office building. It was business like enough, but also had the trappings of a man who was not only the boss but also expressed his power in various ways. It was not long into the conversation that he began to rehearse his final arrival at this pinnacle of success. And it was a rehearsal – sounding as though he had given the speech many times before.

We talked over the business that brought me there, and then I left with the distinct impression that I would not want to be in his way to the top, nor would I want to be him when he finally found that one enemy who would short circuit his quest for power. Years passed by and I met him again. He was much heavier, less well dressed and going into a fast food restaurant that I was coming out of. He recognized me, but started to pass without speaking, until I greeted him and extended my hand. He shook it cautiously and did not allow our eyes to meet. I asked how things were going in the company and with his family. He simple responded that he was no longer there, had made a change in jobs, and was starting over again.

There was something in his voice and manner that was quite uncharacteristic of the person I had met before, so I pressed a bit, asking if he was OK and if there was anything I could do. Tears filled his eyes and he started to just turn and leave, then stopped and confided that he had been fired and had been unemployed for about a year.

Bad things happen in life. Success is never a final plateau from which we rest for the remainder of life. It is a constant journey. The designation of final success can only be assigned to a given event or project, not to the totality of life. Unfortunately, we tend to think of success and failure as a position of stature in life, rather than as a periodic event that we experience on our way through life. The need is to discover life as a journey, punctuated by many events and many circumstances. No one event, good or bad, is able to label us as a success or a failure. In fact, the totality of our life may never be accurately measured by those who look on and in some cases not even by our self.

The problem with our usual evaluation of success and failure is that it is related to position and power and the events that seem to generate them. True success is none of this. It is not the kind of car we drive, the size of the house we live in, the social group we party with or the political influence that we gain. Success, in its true definition has nothing to do with the events, the finances or the status we achieve in life. Success is created by becoming the person I was created to be. It is a matter of becoming rather than a matter of rising through the ranks to a position of power. It is about the journey, not just about one stop on the path.

When Linda and I were much younger and had only been married for a short time, we won a trip for two to Las Vegas. It included room, shows, and a couple of free meals. One of the free luncheons was held in a remote location and was really a sales  pitch to sell desert property far from Las Vegas. Naively, we got on the bus and was transported to this remote spot and fed a quick lunch before the sales grind started. Neither of us was comfortable with the situation and wished we had not won the trip, but we did have to wait it out to get the ride back to our hotel.

Seated with us was an elderly couple, who became the salesman's focus, I presume because they were older and presumably had more money that we newlyweds. The salesman ground away at them, looking for something that would motivate them to buy. Didn't they want to be rich? And they smiled at him and calmly advised that they were very rich. They had their family nearby them, had a nice mobile home and sufficient retirement income to meet their needs. He tried everything to find something in them that desired to make money, get rich, have a second home, increase their inheritance to their children – everything. What he found was a couple who knew who they were, knew what they wanted and had no need to bite into the sales pitch.

Somewhere in the vast opportunities of life there is a place where we overcome the events and the challenges and become comfortable with ourselves and who we are. We do not respond to the events or measure them as success or failure, we simple move through them intent on our own values, our own life calling and our own sense of what is important. Maturity in life is simply arriving at that place of security, not in what I have or in what I have achieved, but in who I am.

That being the case, I cannot measure the events that are not achievements as 'failure.' I've tried many things that have not worked out. I'd be glad to sell you my plans for a number of ventures. You know the drill – we all go through times of miscalculating the market, or get into partnerships that we should not have, or worse, doing wrong things that we knew we should not have. If success is not measured by any event or series of events, than failure is not either. You may have done some really stupid things that everyone around you, including yourself, defines as failure. But the measurements we use are time and place oriented and miss the overall meaning of life. Failure is never fatal.

King David in the Bible was a murder and thief – he stole his neighbor's wife. But that was an event that he paid dearly for, but refused to make the epitaph of his life. Many of our industrial moguls of the past failed in more businesses than they succeeded in, yet we see them through the eyes of the one business that succeeded and remains. If we mark ourselves as having arrived or as having been defeated at any one point in time, we miss the major secret of life. We fail to see life as a journey and as the accumulation of learning experiences upon which I build, not just a personal power base, but a base on which I become what I was created to be. In that view lays the secret to happiness, contentment, peace and ultimate success.

Success is never final, failure is never fatal – courage is what counts. Keep moving!

Chapter 14

Secret #12 – The Universe (& God) is Not Reluctant.

Theology most often reflects what people believe rather than determines what people believe. One of the facts of human reality is that we are not objective – we believe what we want to believe, what we need to believe and what our emotions and personality predispose us to believe.

I will get a lot of disagreement with that statement, for you alone, transcend the rest of frail humanity and you are the last and only objective human alive. (Grin)! Many arguments are pretexted by a statement to show how objective we are and how we are not swayed by circumstance, our history or our desires in fabricating our belief system. So, I will give you the benefit of the doubt and simply say that most people are not objective – only you and possibly me!!!

Of course, all religious groups have a concept of God, and although they differ from group to group, they are mostly similar, with some variations. For most, God is conceived of as all-powerful, everywhere present, and one who knows all things. Most also profile God as reluctant. That's right, reluctant. God does not operate on our wave length, so we cannot know all that He does, we presume, and thus we need to accept that we will not get out of life what we want but rather what God wants for us. Now let me stop here and affirm that I believe that, but there is a subtle twist that seems to have penetrated the human spirit and sets us up to believe that this mysterious plan that God has for us is not going to be good. It might be right for us, but we are not going to like it.

It is here that we need to challenge our thinking and come to grips with our next secret. God is not mischievous although He is often subtle. He is not reluctant although He is not Santa Claus. He created the universe to provide for us and to be the depository of all that we need. What we sometimes fail to understand is that everything that is available to us is already given to us. It is already here.

As a child I often went to prayer meeting in our little church. Few people attended prayer meetings – it was only the faithful, I was told. So, wanting to be good and faithful, I attended. These meetings were something that you could not understand unless you were part of the culture, for people would come into the prayer room, kneel and pray. I think the objective for many was to wear God our and overcome His reluctance. At least that is how it seemed to me in my immaturity. Now that I am older and more mature (check with my wife on this one), I still see it the same way. The language of prayer seemed to be to plead with God to give me something of do something that I was presenting to Him. Now understand, I am in favor of prayer, and I do believe it works, but to the degree that we are attempting to overcome God's reluctance and get Him to do what He is not otherwise pleased to do, I suspect we are wasting a lot of valuable time.

That same basic concept pervades religion and it also pervades life outside of the church house. There seems to be some sort of an assumption that we do not have what we need to have and that there is some power, some force that holds it in trust, waiting for us to do the right thing, push the right button, buy the right lottery ticket or meet the right person. We need to be good or Santa will not bring us a present. But by contrast the news blares out the salary of the professional athlete who has just been jailed for drug use, animal abuse, rape or shooting someone. How is it that they get the money while being bad?

No, being good, although it definitely has long-term advantages, does not overcome, in and of itself, the reluctance of the universe to bring to me what I need. God does not lean over the balcony of human history and say, "I think I'll just mess with all these people and give more to some and others, well, I just down like them much!"

One of the primary principles of theology is that God is no respecter of persons. He does not make those kinds of determinations. He is incapable of mischief. No one is restricted from the universal flow of value. The limiting factor is not in the available resources of the universe or in the determinations of God. The limiting factor is in our own mind and the limitations we place on ourselves.

You cannot overcome God's reluctance – He does not have any! The whole matter of our spending time and energy trying to bargain with the forces of the universe betrays an attitude of insignificance and is self defeating. There is a point of release in which we understand that it is already here.

I was setting in church (I did that a lot as a child) listening to the preacher talk about things, when all of a sudden he said something that cut across my understanding. He said that we tend to form our concept of ourselves based on our view of time. We see our own humanity and measure it as sinful, inadequate, inept, and unworthy simply because of our insecurity and fear. It is that fear-based orientation that makes us constantly plead with God to forgive us, to help us and to do for us. Then he said something that revolutionized my thinking. He said, "It is finished." He began to explain that what God is up to in the work of Calvary, completed the sacrifice for us. There is nothing we can do to become what we already are. Maybe I better say that one again… There is nothing we can do to become what we already are.

You see, if we try to wrestle from the universe what it already provides, it will not do anything and we will get really tired. But, if we approach life as it is, a banquet to be enjoyed, then our efforts take on a whole different dimension and our results are also totally different. It is not in the amount of effort, but in the orientation of our thinking and how we perceive our world. What God did for us is past tense. It is finished and available. What creation holds in store for us is already created and ready for our creative participation. The issue is not overcoming reluctance but in accessing the available.

We tend to look to government to find the right leader, create the right legislation, make a new program, or in some way solve the problems that exist in our land. This is backwards thinking and will not result in anything other than more government. It is  self-perpetuating, this thing we call government. As essential as it may be for our safety and for control of the baser elements of society, it does not create value; it only redistributes value – less governmental costs, of course. Government does not create value – it takes value from us in the form of taxes. It has no intrinsic value in and of itself. Do not wait for the government to solve the world's problems.

Any thinking that looks to another agency to do it for us, whither it is government, the company, God or some cosmic force, is a waste of time and is furthermore a bondage of mind that holds us captive to wrong thinking. We have to rid ourselves of reluctance thinking and raise our understanding to anticipate the available resources that abound around us.

71

Open your hand. That's it, extend your hand and open it in front of you. What is it that lies just outside of your reach, waiting for you to take a hand full? Go ahead... Reach for it. Dream of 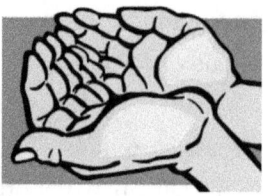 it, plan for it. Set it in motion. Create it. It is already there, already given and already for you to make it yours. If you assume that you have nothing and are worth nothing and the universe is bent on keeping you down, that is where you will be. The inverse is also true. The difference is in your own mind!

Chapter 15

Secret #13 - You are not what you think you are...

Our productivity flows out of our concept of our self. If we believe that we are worthless and inept, we will live accordingly, but if we believe good of our self and can conceive of our holding value in our world, then we will also live that out. What we believe is what we produce. First the thought, the concept and the image, then the fruit of it. The seed always produces after its own kind.

The problem in this sequence of events is in finding a proper image to believe in. What we allow to determine our image is extremely important to our productivity. Most of humanity gets it wrong. Most are sold on some pop psychobabble of self-generated positive imagery that has only a fleeting emotional base. That is, as long as you are pumping yourself up, you are OK, but as soon as the emotion and energy needed to generate that emotional high is gone, you are back to the self doubt, fears and negative programming of the past because there is no substantial basis for the hype.

Let me tell you another story....

She came to the church office, cautious as to my reaction, but filled with resolve in her current quest. She announced that she was leaving her husband and children, the church and was going off to find herself. She expressed regret that she had to do this, but she recounted the years of growing up with the socially implied expectations of her parents, then into an early marriage and the expectations of her husband, then another husband and then a third, and then another, and finally this one and the children, each with their own needs and demands and of the smothering of her life into an endless stream of external impositions and expectations, until she was finally drained, devoid of any personal identity and had become a dull void of a human shell without identity.

I stopped her and asked, "And which psychologist have you been going to?" She laughed and asked me how I knew. I explained that I had also taken the classes and knew the theory, but then asked if I could ask her a couple of questions. She agreed. I asked, "Where are you going in this quest to find yourself?" She replied that she was going to Southern California and didn't know how long she would be there. I commented that it was interesting that when people went away to find themselves, they inevitably went to Southern California, of Hawaii, or some other nice warm climate. "Why is it," I asked, "That no one goes to Iowa, or Alaska or Peoria?" She just looked at me quizzically without an answer.

"Tell me," I asked again, "is it that selves only grow in on a beach, in warm sun and within the sound of the serf? And how will you know yourself, when you find you? Will you be walking along barefoot in the sand and stub you toe on something and look down and discover that, low-and-behold, you have found yourself?" Now she was setting forward on her seat knowing that I was going somewhere and that she still had no answer to the rhetorical questions.

"So," I continued, "what happens if you peel away the lawyers of imposed expectations from your parents, from your husbands, from your children, 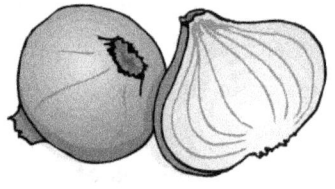 from your church from everyone and find that you are really an onion?" She laughed a nervous laugh, as I continued. "What if when all the layers are removed, behold there is nothing left?

74

What if you discover that you were those lawyers and that absent their context, there is no you?"

I stopped, bid her good-by and walked out with her to her car, stuffed with clothing and personal effects. She said very little, got into her car and left. About a week later she called and said she was miserable and she wished that she had just left town without coming by to let me know what she was doing. She could not stop thinking about what I had said and could not come to grips with the simple stupidity of trying to find something that in effect did not exist. She now wanted some word of wisdom, some counsel, and some direction. I refused. I simply said that I could not solve the dilemma for her, that I had no extra 'selves' lying around to give out. Again she laughed that nervous laugh, then asked what she should do. I waited for a moment and then whispered into the phone, "Selfhood is not found – it is created."

There was a pause and then the question, "But how do I create it? How do I make something I know nothing about? Where should I go to do the work?" She had come to the frustration of searching for that, which can never be found in the quest.

Self is never found, it is created. It does not matter where you are for the place has nothing to do with it. It is an internal construction project with many component parts that are placed together piece by piece to form an identity. But, like to women in my counseling story, most of us do not recognize the process so we just accumulate aimless experiences and influences in our lives without purpose or plan. The end result is a surrealistic image of a person who is neither productive nor happy. Life should never just happen.

How then can life have meaning and how can I understand who I am and what I am to be? These are the basic question of life and the foundation of existence. The answer, I believe,

75

cannot be simply self-generated. Each person was created differently and within the scope of that difference is the key to a unique plan for our life. "We were endowed by our creator with..." Sound familiar? Yes, the framers of our Constitution recognized something about the creative touch that goes into the making of a life. Here then is the key point of identity: You are not what you think you are, you are what God says you are!!!

The core value of human life is found in understanding that mankind was created in the image of God and for creative purpose. We were placed on this planet to create, to subdue and to rule. We are born of the seed of the eternal, endowed with the genius of God Himself and He has already determined good for us. The more I understand about the creator and His purpose for the planet, the more I assimilate my own identity and understand that I am who He says I am, and that is never demeaning, never derogatory and never without high regard.

The problem is in trying to live up to the full potential that has been given to me. Success is becoming what you were created to be – and that is a tall order. Let's look at it from another angle. In most cases we thrash about in life trying to get attention, trying to find significance, trying to be somebody. But if we can shift gears and stop long enough to grasp it, we can come to peace with this simple fact: You cannot become what you already are. Possibly we should say that again. You cannot become what you already are. What you were created to be is in the seed planted in your genetic structure. You can fight with it and doubt it and go off to find it, but you cannot alter it, for it is already there. The seed is there. **You are the seed to be planted.**

Service is the key to definition. The more you find ways to serve humanity and to benefit others out of what you can offer in your creative uniqueness, the more what you are is expressed and defined. When the focus is on defining who I am, the energy is short circuited, but when I can forget about myself and genuinely serve others, I am doing what I was created for – filling my human role in this cosmic mix of human social intercourse. You can develop what you are, and in that sense create yourself, but the seed is already planted – only the refinement of the context remains to give birth to the genius that is yours.

So, how do we go about creating our self? It is a very complex path yet a very simple equation. The path is complex in that it is filled with options, voices demanding our attention and allegiance, people knowing exactly what we should do with our lives, primarily to benefit them. The shouting of the media, advertising and of family and friends can be confusing, unless we are able to find that resting place when we are refreshed in our own sense of who God is and what He has called me to. It is in this higher place that the peace comes that passes understanding and allows me to know what is my talent to be given in service to my world.

There is no marketability for me if I aimless wander through life, searching for myself. Finance flows to those who have a dead certain compass and know what they are doing and why. Productivity is squelched by uncertainty but it is released by a sense of vision and  purpose that attracts people and with that attraction, releases money. Life is not about finding yourself. It is about creating – finding what you are good at, allowing a vision of your potential to wash over your mind and captivate your spirit. You can create good things, you can make the world a better place and you can find the rewards that come with that creative energy.

Be very careful about your self-talk. God never says bad things about His kids. Neither should you. You are what God says you are. Live it out.

Life is an empty canvass on which we create a picture of ourselves. We determine what we are by understanding what God has given to us in talents and abilities and then by our refining them into what we desire and design.

Chapter 16

Secret #14 – Learn to Prune Your Financial Bush

Linda loves to garden. She seems to be able to make anything grow and at times is brutal with her plants. I came home a while back to find the lovely plant she was growing in the kitchen window, cut back to the soil line. I was somewhat shocked, but she had an explanation for it. She was just pruning. Pruning, I thought was just getting rid of some dead branches, not cutting the whole plant down. But, for some reason beyond my understanding, it was gone. Everything green was cut away.

In a few days, low-and-behold, there was some new growth and a round stem rising from the ground where the former leaves had been. In what seemed like days, the stem bloomed and out popped the most beautiful flower I had ever seen. There is a principle in this. Pruning does something even to a fruitful vine. It increases the yield.

Now, it is certainly an over-simplification for me to just say you should cut up your plants. I still do not know how much to cut on the plants and when to do it, but then, that is not our point here. The  point is that agricultural principles have ramification in finance as well. Pruning has value in financial things.

Years ago I worked for General Motors for a brief time as a management consultant. I walked into one of my assigned auto dealerships, intent on dealing with my list of items I needed to go over with the dealer. I always bought a newspaper when I came into town and looked to see what the dealer was doing with advertising and if he had an ad in the help wanted section of the want ads. This would give me a snap shot of his situation and help to direct my attention when I arrived at the business. I was supposed to be the management expert and to advise on how to be more productive. All too often I was the student rather than the teacher.

On this one day I noticed that there was an ad for sales people in the paper, but I thought he had a full sales staff. So when I arrived I asked what was happening with his sales staff. He looked surprised at me and indicated that it was doing fine. So I asked why he was still advertising for more people. He laughed at me and showed me a chart on his desk. It was a typical sales production chart showing each salesperson and their sales for the month. As usual there was a top salesman and then the various others who had sold fewer units, in a scale from the top on down to the one who had sold but a few.

He then revealed to me one of his management principles that I shall never forget. He said that all of life was comprised of our activities within one unchangeable context – time. Time was the measure of all things. It measured our activities, our recreation and our productivity. Everyone has the same amount of it. No one has 25 hours in a day and no one has 23 hours for their day. Everyone gets 24 hours. But some people produce more in their allotted time than others. Some efforts produce more money than others. Some social activities are more enjoyable than others. So, he said he had learned to prune his life. He had learned that in order to do more, he had to cut off some things. He did this, because there are only 24 hours in a day.

Then he showed me the sales chart again. He showed the sales schedule and that everyone was assigned the same amount of floor time as anyone else, but some people used less time to accomplish more, so in order to increase productivity he needed to prune the bottom 10 to 20 % of unproductive people. He did the same with every area of his life. He would stop social activities that he did, simply because they were obligation, opting to go to those events that he truly enjoyed. He did the same with his financial life. He would cut off the bottom several investments or money making activities, even if they were making a profit so he could use the time and money for something that would potentially be more productive. He was a man of lists.... A list for everything!!! But true to his statements, every list had a line drawn through the bottom few items. These were targeted for pruning. They were going to get cut.

I concluded my business and left the dealership, then went to my hotel room and spread out my dealer list. Sure enough, there at the top was the dealer I had just left. He was the top producer and he had far fewer complaints than any of the others. I simply pulled out a pen and went down the list about 85% of the way and drew a line. The bottom few were my target dealers from that point on.

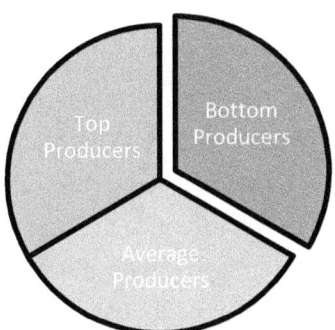

It was an interesting process, but it was far less painless than I thought. I asked two of those dealers if they wanted to sell their franchise. They lit up at the chance to get out of the business that they no longer loved. After interviewing several applicants, I chose two and started their paperwork. They became two of my top dealers. Three other dealers I started spending more time with and taught them this principle and more, borrowing everything I could learn from the better dealers and giving it to them. They responded and started being productive. Things were looking up for my dealers and they were looking up for me. In four years the district I had taken, which was last in the nation in sales per capita moved steadily up to become number one. It was not that I was so smart, or so aggressive, or so efficient. It was that I was really good at one thing: Plagiarism! I stole every principle of success I could find and gave it away to everyone in my district.

Pruning is not just a good principle in gardening or in business. It is a good principle in life. There are tons of things that take our time, sap our strength and steal our joy. We learn to allow them because they serve some kind of purpose for a time, but then they just sort of hang on and stay with us. Like the negative friend that we do not know how to get rid of or the hypercritical relative or the bill for some magazine we never read. There are many things in our world that could use a good pruning occasionally.

But it is not just the external things that keep us from full meaning and effectiveness in life. There are attitudes in us and time traps that are internal that reduce our enjoyment of life and our resources. Pruning them is not the most enjoyable thing we will do in our day, but it may be the most productive.

One of the key question to ask ourselves is, "Does this activity, investment, relationship, (Insert whatever category you choose), measure up to the standards I have for it? Does it contribute anything of value to my life or is it a diversion that needs to be pruned?"

- Now I beg you, not to take this advice out of context. To use that rationale in assessing the worth of your relationship with your child or spouse is missing the point. There are some relationships that we need to improve and give into that are not financial addendums to our life. They are life itself – or should be!

If I am getting out of an investment or business activity what I want, then – leave it alone. But if not, you can't keep doing the same thing over and over and hope it will automatically change for some unknown reason. If you want different results, you have to change what you are doing. The results will not change until the activities change.

We were renting a building for the church some years ago in a business complex. The landlord raised the rent in an attempt to pay for increased costs and it seemed too much for one of the clients, so they changed locations, moving out of their suite. The landlord now had a greater loss of income, so he raised the rent again to cover it. Predictably, another business found it too much, so they moved out also. A third time, the landlord raised the rent, but this time, everyone gave notice. Some courses of action do not give you the results you imagined. If they don't, it might be wise to consider why they did not work, rather than to doggedly continue to do them.

For every action there is an equal and opposite reaction. That is a scientific principle that simple will not change. If you do not like the result you are getting, you need to change the actions that are producing them. Sometimes, you need to be as radical as Linda, and cut the entire plant back to ground level. Who knows! You might find a beautiful flower.

Chapter 17

Secret # 15 - Financial Institutions are not your friend

He sat in front of me smiling and telling me how much insurance I needed. When he finished, I asked for a total of all he had proposed and he hesitated and then began to tell me of the value I was getting for each of the 'products' I was getting and of the small cost per month related to the large pay out should I ever need them. So, I concluded, he was not going to give me a straight answer, so I started writing them down and listing the cost. The end figure was 25% of my monthly income and he was proposing that I spend it on a 'product' called insurance. I told him I'd think about it and he agreed to go away and let me if I agreed he could follow up later with a phone call or a visit.

About a week later he 'stopped by' my office since he was 'in the area' and asked if I was ready to realize the great benefits of his 'products.' I had thought it over and so I started in on him...

I concluded that, although the insurance industry had started using the word 'product,' that he did not have a product to sell me. What he had was a service, or at least it started out to be a service. I painted for him the picture I had in my mind of the origins  of the insurance industry. Long ago and probably far away, a group of rural people (most of our ancestors were agricultural people) decided that occasionally they were not able to join the community barn raising after a neighbor's barn burned down, so they proposed that they could put away a little money each month and help that way. Then others joined, and contributed their share of this pool, insuring that if there were a major loss in their neighborhood, it would have the pool to cover it. Then, some entrepreneurial fellow decided that he could make a business out of setting up the pools, charge a little service fee and make it a company. Thus the insurance company was born. But over time, the concept of managing the available pool of people's money for them shifted, and the company realized that the pool just set there most of the time and that was certainly tempting, so they decided to make what they were doing a 'product' rather than a service and then it would be their money not the people's, so they could spend it.

So, the pool is gone, and when we buy insurance, the illusion that we are putting money aside for a loss later is just that – an illusion. What we pay is a cash cow to the company for their use in their expenses. Ever wonder why insurance companies and banks have such big beautiful buildings?

Now I am not against insurance for major losses. In fact, I have some. But let's get real about the purpose of the companies and their products. They are there to make money, not manage our pool of funds.

Next I explained that we were really adversarial in our relationship. We were on opposite sides of the table. In buying his product, I was betting that I would die soon, or sooner than the premium paid reached as much as the benefit. But he was betting that I would live longer than the value paid out at the end of the policy and pay more in premiums. So like the local casino, the odds were in his favor because he and the company set the premium and made the

charts the premium was based on. So, the picture is of a betting parlor with the odds in the companies favor and we are putting our money on the line based on our perception of the need and the value of the chart. If I could be sure that my life or whatever the insurance is for, was on the average scale, I would be better off putting the money in savings, for the law of averages would say that I would beat the insurance carrier just as they are betting to beat me if I buy their product. You see, they know the averages, so they take the gamble, making sure the odds are in their favor, add a little bit (maybe more than a little bit) on top to pay for overhead and start the clock ticking toward the maturity of my policy. They seldom loose.

Banks do the same thing in a different way. They hold our money and pay us interest on our savings. But the money is not really there, it is loaned out by the bank to others. The difference is, they charge more interest than they pay, so they make a profit. This is not a problem, and we all understand that this happens. There is nothing illegal in the insurance product or the bank service. What it does however is create an illusion that our relationship with the bank or the insurance company is to our benefit. The fact is, they are not giving money to us, they are using our money to make money for themselves. Now to the degree that we need their service, this is not a problem and we are getting what we pay for, but rest assured, we are paying for it. Financial institutions do not feed us, clothes us or buy our gas. They hold our money and make more money and keep the profits.

How we think about our relationship to financial institutions is important for it guides us in determining how much of our money we want them to use for their self. It is financially best to limit the amount and kind of insurance we have and the amount of money we keep in the bank.

It is also important how we think about our government and their services. It is quite common for people to think about the government as having all the money in that they print it after all – don't they? And the answer is, no! NO! NOOOOO! The government does not have any money. When the government prints money it is released into the private sector through the federal banking system. It does not go into the federal bank account to pay federal bills. The government has no money of its own. It gets its money from we the people. The government lives on taxes and investments.

So, when the local politician tells us how much of the federal budget they have gotten for us, they are telling us how much money they are taking from us. The preamble to the Constitution of the United State says, *"We the People of the United States, in Order to form a more perfect Union, establish Justice, insure*

domestic Tranquility, provide for the common defense, promote the general Welfare, and secure the Blessings of Liberty to ourselves and our Posterity, do ordain and establish this Constitution for the United States of America."

The scope and purpose of government was to be very narrow and very specific. Much of what our government is now doing is not within the scope of these narrow purposes. What government should be about is protecting our liberties and defending its people. What it ends up doing is redistributing the wealth of the people who earned it. Every program that is designed to help some unfortunate segment of our society has to be funded. It not only needs the money it is going to give away on the program, it needs the money to administer the program. In many cases, the government bureau that is created to help someone eats up 90 to 110% of the funds.

Now again, it is not a problem that the government takes care of things that we need taken care of, but how we think about it is important. The tendency is to vote for the politician who promises us the most benefits as though they were going to reach into their pocket to give those benefits. But they are not and cannot. They are reaching into our pockets to give us whatever it is that we want and they are going to create an administrative bureau to watch over it. The benefit is going to cost us up to 200% of its value if we have the government do it for us. Yet, each election we seem to revel in the promises of those who are going to give us more. How we think about this is important to our financial health.

A good way to look at the institutions that cost us money is to see first of all, that they do. They do cost us money. Therefore, the less we use them the better off we are. If we can self-insure, loan our money directly, or not get government services, we benefit financially. What I am not advocating is a separation from government, not having insurance or not using the banking services. What I am advocating is correcting our thinking so that we are not blindly paying money for and to institutional services that do not in fact benefit us financially, but take money away from us.

It's your money! Keep all you can!

Chapter 18

Secret #16 – What you get will not satisfy.

One of the illusions of our Western Culture is that the accumulations of material good will satisfy us. In contrast, some of the Eastern philosophies are given more to introspective pursuits and focus away from the material advantages of our Western lives. While the historical setting for the development of worldviews is quite different, to some degree, the philosophy of life can be seen as a reflection of the cultural and economic setting in which the worldview developed.

While Twentieth Century America and Europe have been primarily focused on development, progress and the production of wealth, much of the rest of the world was focused on mere survival. These contrasting settings give rise to differing realities, each woven carefully with corresponding views of the world around us and the world of the future. Each attempts to incorporate the given reality of the moment into some sort of philosophy of life that make sense and provides meaning.

One of the difficult parts of making sense of our Western materialistic frame of reference is the seeming spiritual and emotional emptiness that exists inside of the materialistic mind. The question is, are the wealthy happier than the poor? The answer is not easy to determine, for who knows what is really going on inside of anyone else's mind. Against many critics of our materialistic world, some studies seem to indicate that the rich are more satisfied with their lives than the poor. But, the argument of what is the right worldview and what is the right way to look at our material progress is one that may not end any time soon.

I certainly do not hope to end that debate in one catchy phrase, but I do think it is possible to transcend the arguments of conflicting realities, and deal with the issues that we all face in finding meaning and being productive in our world. And those are some of the basic issues of life: Meaning and being productivity. The illusion that we are sold in advertising is that by having certain things, we will be happy. Our commercial appeal is to be slim, pretty, sexy, and stylish and have the latest things. But purchasing is different from making. To buy ones way into acceptance, love or good relationships is an illusion sold to us daily on TV, the Internet, or the daily paper. We are told visually, and in so many words, that if you buy a certain car, or use a certain toothpaste, or take a certain pill or wear a certain brand label or... And on it goes. Happiness, we are told, is in attaining a certain kind of status.

Ah, but our experience tells us differently. You can put the pig in the right clothes and the right jewelry and into the right car, and it is still a pig. The external symbols of success do not success make. We are not our  clothes, our cars, our houses, or our projected imagery. We are who we are, and nothing more; and − nothing less! Happiness is not determined by the image I project but by the person I become. We are rewarded, in the most basic and real sense, not by image, but by character, by integrity and by what we are able to give into the relationships that surround us.

Thus, life is not about arriving at some fanciful place of political power or by the accumulation of stuff, but by the way in which I make the journey and what I produce from my skill set into the world around me, while on the way. Life is not about the arrival. It is about the journey. It is about becoming what I was created to be. It is about the fulfillment of those basic instincts of creativity, production and giving of self into the world. Satisfaction is found more in giving than in having. The interesting thing is, they who live life to the full tend to benefit from their creative fulfillment and their sharing of their genius with the world. What you invest into the world comes back to you. If you sow, you will reap. The inevitable law of harvest works in agriculture and in every other endeavor of life.

Developing what you are and learning to love life rather than things. Enjoy the journey, for in the end, that is all there is. Life is not a rehearsal.

Chapter 19

Producer or Consumer?

We are told that wealth is measured by assets minus liabilities. That is the common and accepted way that accounting is done. But I want to object to this as too simplistic and lacking in definition. I propose that it is possible to have tons of assets and still be poor. Let me explain...

George and Ellen were fine young people who just happened to be the grand son and grand daughter-in-law to a wealthy manufacturing tycoon. The old man died and left them a fortune by any standard. They were sad that granddad had passed away, but not sad that they were named in the will. They were off and running. They bought a new house in an exclusive neighborhood in town, bought a new boat, motorhome, furniture, cars, and all of the things that made them appear as rich as they were. They then started traveling and loved to go to Las Vegas and stay in the suites reserved for high-rollers. Life was great.

But, they were accumulating, what their accountant would say were depreciating assets. Sure enough, within about 5 years the money was gone and so were all the symbols of wealth as the law of depreciating consumables took over and someone else had the asset value of the estate they had squandered. Read the myriad accounts of those who have hit the lottery or some other big casino win. For the most part it is the story of tragedy as the money goes sliding away, into what appears to be tangible assets, but over time, depreciation and waste deduces it all to nothing.

Having assets and things that money can buy is not wealth. It may hold the appearance of wealth but appearances are fragile and often illusions. Wealth, real long term personal wealth, is not determined by what you can buy but by what you produce. This measure reduces the world to two kinds of people - those who produce wealth and those who consume it. If it is only consumed, it will vanish as one eats through the base assets with the ravenous appetite for things. Things do not maintain wealth, only continued productivity does.

Those who focus on productivity and creating something for the use of others will be continuously renewing their asset value as time goes on. Those who focus on accumulating things will end up giving over their wealth to those that they buy from. This, regardless of their original asset value, will depreciate if they are not supported by a continuous restoration of the wealth that they came from. The renewal of value comes from creative productivity. If we retire from producing we not only die from boredom, we also set in motion the raiding of our wealth by being a consumer rather than a producer.

Most people in our world consume all that they make and set their eyes on a job that gives them enough to meet their weekly budget. They become trapped on the treadmill of working hard enough to make ends meet and producing enough to make it through the week. This kind of existence leaves us one crisis or one illness away from financial collapse.

The alternative to that is to determine to produce more than you need and to market the rest. It is this kind of mind-set that drives the economy and reveals our creative genius. Somewhere, in every one of us is an idea, a product, a service or a challenge that will open to us the door of productivity and a stream of wealth. The focus is not on what you can buy and what symbols of wealth you can set in your driveway but on what is the talent and abilities God has give you to develop and to use in being productive in life.

If you set in front of the TV for many hours you will see all of the products that you should not live without. Success and sexuality is determined, or so advertisers would have us believe, by the products we buy and the consumables that we have. Wrong! Dead Wrong! The happy person is not the one with the most toys but the one who is doing what they were created to do and producing that which only they can contribute to the world. The producer always rules the consumer.

And, the status we have in this chain of producing and consuming is not determined by fate or chance. It is a decision we make in the ordered plan we have

Our station in life is a choice.

for our life. Our station in life is a choice. It is chosen by our willingness to see ourselves differently from the masses and to order our time, energy and activity in finding that which we can give into life and to enhance others who need us. There is nothing evil in producing something of value and charging for it! Nothing evil at all.

Chapter 20

The Law of Supply

There is no shortage of supply in terms of available resources. There is more than enough for all. Shortages are created just as abundance is created. The supply chain is simply a system of the flow of value that has been created by those who do productive enterprise. Additions to that flow are not prohibited but are in fact welcomed. The greatest growing segments of our economy are evidence that anyone can step into the stream and market their creative genius.

The visible supply of productivity is virtually endless, and yet, there remains an invisible supply that has not yet been envisioned and created that is greater by far than the visible. There is room for you and your ideas in the marketplace of added value. Everything you see in the marketplace is made from the original creation of the planet and out of that, all things proceed. New forms are constantly being created, and older ones are passing away. New business are starting and replacing old ones as creativity is expanding on old ideas and creating new ones. There is no limit to the  supply nor to the creativity that goes into new products and services.

No one is poor because nature is poor or because there is not enough to go around. God did not limit His creation to the original form of the resources of the earth. That is both obvious and certain. Nature is an inexhaustible storehouse of riches. The supply will never run out. And there is no limit to the ideas and creative energy that produces the forms and productive values that can be created from the resources of the planet.

New wealth forms come out of creativity applied to the resources of the earth as the needs of mankind are met and new ideas come into the marketplace. The shortage, if there is any, is in the ideas on what to do and how to do it. That shortage is solved by creative people casting off the mind-set of limitation and rejecting the voices of limitation.

Look at the list of things that simply did not exist 100 years ago. Think of the economic arenas of enterprise that did not exist 20 years ago. Think of the new and emerging areas of scientific advancement that are now in their infancy and think of the vast array of support services that will be demanded as they surface in the economy of tomorrow. We are on the verge of the greatest economic and scientific revolution ever in the history of mankind, while prophets of doom stand by telling us the earth is at the end of its resources.

The universe is a living entity, always inherently moving toward life. That is how it was created - life begetting life. Creation was formed for the perpetuation of life and is motivated by the creator to increase and fill up the earth. God does not contradict Himself by limiting that which He set in motion by the laws of abundance.

The response of the ideas and resources of nature are available to anyone who will recognize them and access them. They are inanimate, seeking a human source to activate them and work them into a product or service. Again, the world and its resources is not the problem. The problem is the mind-set of humanity.

One of the great barriers to our success and creativity is the political process that has evolved on our planet. We elect those who promise to give us things and take care of us. In order to get our vote, they define problems for us that they will solve if elected. Sometimes, that involves setting up the image of a crisis, a shortage or of world devouring global warming, cooling, shaking or other near extinction event that they will stop if elected. But the end result of the process is that we buy into the pictures of doom that they create and vote in the worst possible candidates who license, limit and tax creativity and resourcefulness. The best thing we can do is to ignore their limited minds and vote for the lazy politician who promises to go to the capitol and play golf, allowing us the freedom to explore, create and develop the productivity of which we are capable.

Chapter 21

The Theory of a Limited Pie

The basic concept of a socialistic construct, whither it is collectivism, communism or any other form of socialism, is that we have a limited pie from which we all take a share. If I take a bigger piece of the pie than others, then I am immoral and stealing what is rightfully theirs.

If we look back at our statistics of the growth in world population then, that, in and of itself, should show that concept to be in error. The fact is, those who add value to the pie, increase its size. Our economy is not a fixed base figure but expands and contracts with the  degree of value that goes into it. By creating, producing and inventing you do not just shift wealth within the limited pie but increase the size of the pie.

This is a difficult concept for the socialist mind to grasp. Their need to see equality for all obscures the sense of opportunity that exists for all. Everyone can create wealth. No one is restricted from doing so. There is no balancing mechanism that says that my increase takes its value away from anyone. That is true in the distribution of resources, talent, creativity, and for the wealth that flows to any new idea or product. There are no limits.

Let's look at that phenomenon from a practical example for a minute. It we were to go backward in time to a point before the technological revolution that we now enjoy, and remember that there was no Microsoft, Intel, Apple, Adobe, HP, Gateway, Genentech, Sun Micro, Argus Holdings, Alert ID, and a thousand others. Where was all of the value and money that they now represent? Did the emergence of these companies create poverty everywhere they sprang up? Nonsense. They created prosperity everywhere they sprang up. Growth is good for the economy. Creativity does not rob the poor, it enhances their prospects of getting in on the creative growth of yet another harvest from the fields of human ingenuity.

The pie shrinks when it is not fed new advances and creative energy. In increases when it is. You cannot solve the problems of the poor by restricting the creativity of those who produce wealth. You cannot save the economy or the world condition by trying to equal out the size of each piece of the economy. Equality, as a concept, applies to basic human worth and should include the opportunity to excel in life. It does not guarantee that each individual will apply themselves to education, the energy of applying themselves to a task or to the developing of creative genius. To keep the creative and energetic down and to penalize them for what they do, does nothing to lift those who do not.

Life is a banquet, filled with wonderful dreams, exciting possibilities and wonderful creations, ready to be explored and taken hold of. The fact that not everyone comes to the table should never mean that we should destroy

the table. Envy of the creative does not make me more creative, in fact, it only secures to me an excuse for not altering my course and doing life differently so that I also become a productive contributor to the size of the pie.

Do not envy the rich and productive - emulate them. Never look down on the poor or disregard their state. The best way to help them is to not become one of them. The second best way to help them is to show them how to move beyond their self imposed limitations. Poverty is a trap of the mind that strips people of their hopes, dreams, energy, potential and the sense of possibilities that belong to all of us. Encouragement and motivation are of more value that a dollar in the beggars cup.

"You cannot help the poor by destroying the rich.

You cannot strengthen the weak by weakening the strong.

You cannot bring about prosperity by discouraging thrift.

You cannot lift the wage earner up by pulling the wage payer down.

You cannot further the brotherhood of man by inciting class hatred.

You cannot build character and courage by taking away people's initiative and independence.

You cannot help people permanently by doing for them, what they could and should do for themselves."
Abraham Lincoln

Chapter 22

Training Your Genius

One of the great frustrations of my life has been the piano. I love the music produced by a good piano from the hands of a skilled artist, but my early interest in the piano found me pecking out a tune, note at a time with no accompanying chords. Just as it took years to learn to walk, so also it took years to learn to play the piano. The music was in there - in my head, but I had an inability to translate that music onto the keyboard. I still love piano music and, although the interest and talent for playing may be there, I still fight to make it come out of my hands, for my life pursuits did not include a serious pursuit of playing the piano.

This is true for all of life. Success is not found in just having an interest or a thought, but in the willingness to pursue that thought and interest with all of your might. There is a great story of the old master violin player, who was  approached by the young man after the concert. The Young man asked, "How do you play like that? I would give everything to be able to play like that." The old master smiled wisely at him and said, "That is exactly what it will take to do it."

Interest in something is easy. Having a creative thought is also easy in that most of us have quite a few ingenious thoughts over our lifetime. But focusing in on one and pursuing it until it is planned, formed, developed and released into the marketplace is another thing. All too many wonderful and ingenious creations never become a product or service for lack of learning how to do it and how to place it in the market. The idea is simply the starting point. Action from that point through completion is usually the essential missing item.

Training and developing the thought takes time. It is no different than training your body to walk in early childhood. There are many falls and many failures along the way. But in fact, they are not failures, just successful experiments in learning how not to use your body to walk. It is sometimes a process of elimination. Don't be discouraged by trying and not finding immediate success. You are learning along the way and will find, in the end, the way to make it work.

Stories are told of Thomas Edison, Benjamin Franklin, Bill Lear, and many others, who worked feverishly toward a desired end result, and waded through multiple years and ways in which they learned they could not produce their product. But they did end up with a working product and blessed the world by spending the time and energy to finish the product. If you have a spark of genius, it will probably take some time, possibly some money and  certainly some training to get it done. To assume that what you have thought of will just magically happen is short sighted. To understand that anything can be done and then to find the way is the metal that genius is made of.

The key to action is to develop an action plan, breaking the task down into component parts so that each step is clear, defined and achievable. If you want to be a brain surgeon, you do not start with a knife sharpening class. Best to start medical school and work your way along the plan. Action is always easier if you can see how component parts of the process interrelate and how to get from where you are to where you are going. But be careful to not get discouraged in the process. The plan will need revision along the way for as your understanding increases, so the definition of where you are going will need to adjust also. Being flexible is important but being persistent in action is the means by which any thought is translated into an end result.

The fact that you do not achieve instant success does not mean that you will never succeed. It only means that you are not finished with the process yet. Everything is a process. Life does not happen all of a sudden.. It unfolds day by day, step by step. Patience is an essential ingredient as long as it does not become laziness and sloth. Patience is a virtue when it accompanies a commitment to see the task through to the end.

Never assume that all you have to do is think about it. You have to get started, keep moving and never stop trying to get it done. Success is the end result of many component parts. Action is what gets you from one step to the other until you finally arrive at your destination.

It is essential to understand the time line for action also. You cannot act in the past. You cannot act in the future. You cannot act where you have been or where you will be. You can only act now. If the actions of the past did not work, forget them. You cannot relive yesterday. But you can make today different than  yesterday by continuing to act now. You cannot wait for the ideal time to act or the right environment for action. Action is not subservient to anything else and it is not conditional on anything else. Action will create the environment and make the time right. The popular catch phrase of today really does have value: Just Do It!.

Successful action is cumulative in its results. Each step leads to another and the accumulation of each successful step adds us to a successful whole. Progress is not made in one sweeping event, but in the accumulation of successful parts. Break it down into steps and then act through the steps and the end result will be a successful whole.

Chapter 23

Attitude is Everything

The difference between the rich and the poor is the attitude. We have all met the brilliant poor man and the ignorant rich man. Intelligence, although it plays a part in what we do and become, is not the primary ingredient in economic success. It is entirely possible to be poor, smart and educated all at the same time.

The difference is often simply in the perception of life and of how nature produces. Some people can plant and harvest and receive a hundred fold increase on their investment seed without any education as to how to do it. They simply have a sense of how nature works. They plant with the expectation of increase, tend the crop and reap the reward.

Others, may well know what to do and how to do it but they do not do so, and they receive no reward. It is not a matter of intelligence entirely, but of the will and actions that come from our attitude. There are different attitudes available to us in all circumstances. Circumstances do not determine the end result but the attitude within the circumstances that makes the final determination.

As I am writing, our nation and our world is in a trying time. The economy of the nation has, for all intents and purposes, flat lined. Some of our states are factually bankrupt without having declared it to the courts as yet. Unemployment is at an all time high and for the first time in recent history, property, which has traditionally been held as the base line of all wealth, has drastically depreciated in value. It is possible to look at any given industry and to declare that this is a time when we are the victim of governmental ineptness and error. Government policy, banking greed, personal ignorance and many other factors have all played into a time of financial collapse.

But that need not be the epitaph of those who see beyond the immediate into the future and into the possibilities that lie ahead. Attitude now will determine the results later and right now there are people who are stimulated to build new businesses, chart new courses and explore great creative dreams. The attitude will determine the end result, not the circumstance itself. The circumstance wins only as we succumb to it and allow the negative messages to rule our minds.

Attitude Determines Destiny!

There are options in the world of attitude, that we can adopt in response to the circumstance of life. And this is true now as it has been in the past and will always be in the future. Attitude determines destiny.

1. Defeat - The Victim

For some, the attitude is of defeat. These people see themselves as the victim or others who have greater power over their lives than they do themselves. They are powerless to do anything but to live out the tyranny of the powerful who have thoughtlessly determined defeat for them. They are hopeless, without a hope, without a plan and without any view of a road out of their state.

Every attitude has a place to generate power. For the victim, the power becomes blame. Someone else is at fault for their state. And, in defense of those who are living with this attitude, there are enough ignorant businesses and politicians to focus the blame on. And they are each deserving of that blame. The

106

problem is, blame focused uses the power that is needed to get out of the hopelessness and consumes the vision and energy of success.

Ultimately, who did what to whom doesn't matter! Blame has to go for progress to begin!

In order to get out of defeat, we have to get rid of blame. As long as I am the victim of any person, system or circumstance, then I am powerless to get out because I am held their by blame. Blame is the jail of poverty and the drain into which power goes that can be used otherwise once it is identified. The problem here is, blame is a comfortable and convenient way of self justifying our condition. But, to get out of the pit of defeat, blame has to go.

2. Passive - Seeking solitude within the pain

Another available attitude in difficult circumstances is to passively accept the state and to seek solitude within the pain. For many, they do not blame others except possibly God, feeling that this is their lot in life and that destiny or God has placed them in this lot, and that the only response is to learn to live with it or perhaps enjoy it as much as one can. Sometimes this passive response to the difficulties of life is the most difficult as those who choose this attitude have lost the desire to grow, change and better themselves. They see no potential in themselves and no need to think, dream, grow or create. They are essentially dead to life but biologically animate, none-the-less. They are content with misery.

Much of human history reflects religious teaching and philosophical perspectives that deal with accepting ones lot in life. While to some degree, we all need to learn contentment and appreciation for what we do have, to bury ones head in the sand and not develop one's self and the God given creativity that is there, is sad indeed. We are not planted on this earth to endure it but to delight in it and to rule over the nature placed in our care. There is genius in every person to be developed and expressed and enjoyed, not only by that one person but by everyone who comes into contact with them. The discovery of that talent and genius is the greatest joy of living.

3. Aggressive - Going to War Against the Circumstance

For some, anger takes over when circumstances are bad and the power is directed into an angry response. That anger will become destructive to others around the person holding it or it will ultimately destroy the person holding it. Anger is an acid, born  of fear and destined to burn its way through any context around it. It is the agent of conflict and the director of terror. It is seldom productive, being bent on being destructive. It strikes out against the circumstance, or so it would seem, but in fact cannot see the circumstance clearly, so it strikes out at people within the same circumstance. Others become the enemy and are blamed for the circumstance. But where the victim succumbs to the circumstance by blaming others, aggressions moved out to confront, not the circumstance, but other people. The end result is damage, usually more so to the person striking out than to those who are initially focused on.

4. Confidence - Finding the Path Out

There is an alternative response to the above attitudes when circumstances are bad. It is to understand that the circumstances are created by human ignorance and that they are not permanent nor are they necessarily terminal. They are simply unintended consequences of human failure. No one really wanted the consequences, they just failed to see them coming.

Somewhere, in the dark forest of fear and the foggy gray of difficulty, is a path to sunlight. It is usually not paved in gold, but may be itself dusty and without perfect definition. But it has signposts of hope and arrows of possibility. It may mean moving against the crowd, seeing things differently than the prevailing media and it may lead to vistas of dreams beyond the normal. It may give rise to a voice of reason and a call to possibilities beyond the experience of the now. It may be unpopular and questioned as to its sanity. But it is the road less traveled by those who are in despair and those who have become victims to the now. It may be the road to Calvary, but it is the road out.

Take it. Walk against the grain of the rest of the world, but do not fear. This path will be uphill and ill-defined at first but it will level off and become wider and more defined as you move along. In the end, it will consume your energy and give back to you power, for on it there are visions of possibility and creative places to inspire your journey. In the end, the darkness and fog will dissipate as the vision of who you are and what you are to do take over the fear and uncertainty and you arrive home - where life is what it was intended to be.

Epilogue

This little book could go on and on, dissecting common attitudes about money, life, and the realities that we assume without challenge. But, in all fairness to the reader and to the author, all things must come to an end.

The intended end of this treatise, is not that the reader should put it down and assess its value as entertainment, but that the reader begin a journey...

May that journey take you into a quizzical mindset that allows you the freedom to challenge your own beliefs and the assumptions you live by. And may it also become a quest to find in the maze of expert opinion and writings available in our world, the truth hidden in the assumptions of others, for without the ability to question and sort through the presumptions of yourself and others we are doomed to continue to repeat the results of the past.

May the journey be met with enthusiasm and hope and never become an intimidating task of despair. Life is far too short to get bogged down in self-doubts, fears, and to get locked up in the cocoon of inaction.

May the journey find you developing simple ways of rejecting ideas that defeat and adapting realities that add to the growth and fulfillment of life. This will take courage, for in rejecting some ideas, the people who hold them may feel rejected as well. While that is never our objective, it is, unfortunately, sometimes the result.

If you have that vague feeling that you were placed on this earth for some purpose and have not yet found it, rest assured you can and you will. The fulfillment of that purpose is not found in an aimless and endless search but in the dedicated creation of who you are.

You are very important to the scheme and purpose of the world. Don't cheat the world out of what it will receive, if you realize your highest and best. Go and dream. Go and create. Go and become!

The author

APPENDIX

The following are provided for your enjoyment, humor and contemplation. The lists are necessarily incomplete, and not verified as to the source to which they are attributed.

We hope that you will enjoy an occasional look at them as you discover more of the wisdom of the ages and find in them secrets to stimulate your creativity.

Quotes From the Ancients

A bird in the hand is worth two in the bush. Latin Proverb

New day, new fate. Bulgarian

One who waits for chance, may wait a year. African

Opportunities come but do not linger. Nepalese

Seneca 4 B.C. 65 A.D., philosopher

It is not because things are difficult that we do not dare; it is because we do not dare that things are difficult.

Everything hangs on one's thinking.

Retire into yourself as much as possible. Associate with people who are likely to improve you. Welcome those whom you are capable of improving. The process is a mutual one. People learn as they teach.

Away with the world's opinion of you—it's always unsettled and divided.

If you shape your life according to nature, you will never be poor; if according to people's opinions, you will never be rich.

You can only acquire it successfully if you cease to feel any sense of shame.

Fortune can take away riches, but not courage.

It is not because things are difficult that we do not dare; it is because we do not dare that they are difficult.

Economy is too late when you are at the bottom of your purse.

There is no delight in owning anything unshared.

If thou art a man, admire those who attempt great things, even though they fail.

Not how long, but how well you have lived is the main thing.

We are more often frightened than hurt; and we suffer more from imagination than from reality.

Where the fear is, happiness is not.

Freedom is not being a slave to any circumstance, to any constraint, to any chance; it means compelling Fortune to enter the lists on equal terms.

He who is brave is free.

Our plans miscarry because they have no aim. When a man does not know what harbor he is making for, no wind is the right wind.

See not how many are better off than you are, but consider how many are worse.

True happiness is to enjoy the present, without anxious dependence upon the future, not to amuse ourselves with either hopes or fears but to rest satisfied with what we have, which is sufficient, for he that is so wants nothing. The great blessings of mankind are within us and within our reach. A wise man is content with his lot, whatever it may be, without wishing for what he has not.

Who can hope for nothing, should despair for nothing.

Most men ebb and flow in wretchedness between the fear of death and the hardship of life; they are unwilling to live, and yet they do not know how to die.

A well governed appetite is the greater part of liberty.

The approach of liberty makes even an old man brave.

Fidelity purchased with money, money can destroy.

If you live according to the dictates of nature, you will never be poor; if according to the notions of man, you will never be rich.

The mind is a matter over every kind of fortune; itself acts in both ways, being the cause of its own happiness and misery.

Quotes From Our Founding Fathers (and others!)

Out of adversity comes opportunity. Ben Franklin

"Government's view of the economy could be summed up in a few short phrases: If it moves, tax it. If it keeps moving, regulate it. And if it stops moving, subsidize it" Ronald Reagan

"I, however, place economy among the first and most important republican virtues, and public debt as the greatest of the dangers to be feared." Thomas Jefferson

"Economists are pessimists: they've predicted 8 of the last 3 depressions" Barry Asmus

The economy depends about as much on economists as the weather does on weather forecasters."

"An economy hampered by restrictive tax rates will never produce enough revenue to balance our budget, just as it will never produce enough jobs or enough profits" John Fitzgerald Kennedy

According to the Bank of England the economy is growing too fast so interest rates must rise to counter the supposed inflationary threat. In lay terms, I interpret this to mean that people are working much harder, causing economic growth, and they're in danger of spending their money, which is what the recession-hit shops want them to do. But the Bank and the City seem to think this is wrong, and that if people work harder they should be punished by having their mortgages increased. Harry Enfield

An economist is someone who knows more about money than the people who have it. Anonymous

An economist's guess is liable to be as good as anybody else's. Will Rogers

Ask five economists and you'll get five different explanations? six if one went to Harvard. Edgar R. Fiedler

Commerce changes the fate and genius of nations. Thomas Gray

Genius changes the fate and commerce of nations. David Fritsche

Approximately 80% of our air pollution stems from hydrocarbons released by vegetation, so let's not go overboard in setting and enforcing tough emission standards from man-made sources. Ronald Reagan

Don't be afraid to see what you see. Ronald Reagan

Entrepreneurs and their small enterprises are responsible for almost all the economic growth in the United States. Ronald Reagan

Government always finds a need for whatever money it gets. Ronald Reagan

Government does not solve problems; it subsidizes them. Ronald Reagan

How do you tell a communist? Well, it's someone who reads Marx and Lenin. And how do you tell an anti-Communist? It's someone who understands Marx and Lenin. Ronald Reagan

There are no great limits to growth because there are no limits of human intelligence, imagination, and wonder. Ronald Reagan

There is a very easy way to return from a casino with a small fortune: go there with a large one. Jack Yelton

I am opposed to millionaires, but it would be dangerous to offer me the position. ~Mark Twain

After a visit to the beach, it's hard to believe that we live in a material world. ~Pam Shaw

A bank is a place that will lend you money if you can prove that you don't need it. ~Bob Hope

Scriptures About Money, Success, Attitude

Proverbs 6:6-8
Go to the ant, sluggard; consider her ways and be wise; who having no guide, overseer, or ruler, provides her food in the summer and gathers her food in the harvest.

Proverbs 21:5

The thoughts of the diligent tend only to plenty; but the thoughts of everyone who is hasty only to poverty.

Proverbs 22:3

A prudent one foresees the evil and hides himself, but the simple pass on and are punished.

Proverbs 24:3-4

Through wisdom a house is built, and by understanding it is established; and by knowledge the rooms shall be filled with all precious and pleasant riches.

Proverbs 25:28

He who has no rule over his own spirit is like a broken down city without a wall.

Proverbs 27:12

A prudent man sees evil and hides himself, the naive proceed and pay the penalty.

Proverbs 27:23

Know well the face of your flocks; and pay attention to your herds.

Proverbs 27:26

The lambs are for your clothing, and the goats are the price of the field.

Luke 14:28-30

For which of you, intending to build a tower, does not sit down first and count the cost, whether he may have enough to finish it;

lest perhaps, after he has laid the foundation and is not able to finish, all those seeing begin to mock him, saying, This man began to build and was not able to finish.

Leviticus 19:13
You shall not oppress your neighbor, nor rob him. The wages of a hired man are not to remain with you all night until morning.

Deuteronomy 25:13-15
You shall not have in your bag differing weights, a large and a small. You shall not have in your house differing measures, a large and a small. You shall have a full and just weight; you shall have a full and just measure, that your days may be prolonged in the land which the LORD your God gives you.

Job 31:13-14
"If I have despised the claim of my male or female slaves when they filed a complaint against me, what then could I do when God arises? And when He calls me to account, what will I answer Him?"

Psalm 112:5
It is well with the man who deals generously and lends, who conducts his affairs with justice.

Proverbs 10:4
Poor is he who works with a negligent hand, but the hand of the diligent makes rich.

Proverbs 11:1
A false balance is an abomination to the LORD, but a just weight is His delight.

Proverbs 13:4

The soul of the sluggard craves and gets nothing, but the soul of the diligent is made fat.

Proverbs 13:11

Wealth obtained by fraud dwindles, but the one who gathers by labor increases it.

Proverbs 16:8

Better is a little with righteousness than great income with injustice.

Proverbs 22:16

He who oppresses the poor to make more for himself or who gives to the rich, will only come to poverty.

Jeremiah 22:13

Woe to him who builds his house without righteousness and his upper rooms without justice, who uses his neighbor's services without pay and does not give him his wages.

Malachi 3:5

Then I will draw near to you for judgment; and I will be a swift witness against the sorcerers and against the adulterers and against those who swear falsely, and against those who oppress the wage earner in his wages, the widow and the orphan, and those who turn aside the alien and do not fear Me, says the LORD of hosts.

Luke 16:10

He who is faithful in a very little thing is faithful also in much;

and he who is unrighteous in a very little thing is unrighteous also in much.

Ephesians 6:9
And masters, do the same things to them, and give up threatening, knowing that both their Master and yours is in heaven, and there is no partiality with Him.

Colossians 4:1
Masters, grant to your slaves justice and fairness, knowing that you too have a Master in heaven.

1 Timothy 5:18
For the Scripture says, "Do not muzzle the ox while it is treading out the grain," and "The worker deserves his wages."

James 5:4
Look! The wages you failed to pay the workmen who mowed your fields are crying out against you. The cries of the harvesters have reached the ears of the Lord Almighty.

Exodus 23:12
Six days do your work, but on the seventh day do not work, so that your ox and your donkey may rest and the slave born in your household, and the alien as well, may be refreshed.

Proverbs 12:11
He who tills his land will have plenty of bread, but he who pursues worthless things lacks sense.

Proverbs 13:11

Wealth obtained by fraud dwindles, but the one who gathers by labor increases it.

Proverbs 13:11

Dishonest money dwindles away, but he who gathers money little by little makes it grow.

Proverbs 14:15

The naive believes everything, but the sensible man considers his steps.

Proverbs 19:2

Also it is not good for a person to be without knowledge, and he who hurries his footsteps errs.

Proverbs 21:5

The plans of the diligent lead surely to advantage, but everyone who is hasty comes surely to poverty.

Proverbs 23:4

Do not weary yourself to gain wealth, cease from your consideration of it.

Proverbs 28:19-20

He who tills his land will have plenty of food, but he who follows empty pursuits will have poverty in plenty. A faithful man will abound with blessings, but he who makes haste to be rich will not go unpunished.

Proverbs 15:22

Without consultation, plans are frustrated, but with many counselors they succeed.

Proverbs 24:27

Prepare your work outside and make it ready for yourself in the field; afterwards, then, build your house.

Proverbs 28:20

A faithful man will abound with blessings, but he who makes haste to be rich will not go unpunished.

Proverbs 13:11

Wealth obtained by fraud dwindles, but the one who gathers by labor increases it.

Proverbs 19:2

Also it is not good for a person to be without knowledge, and he who hurries his footsteps errs.

Ecclesiastes 11:2

Divide your portion to seven, or even to eight, for you do not know what misfortune may occur on the earth.

Matthew 25:14-30

"For it is just like a man about to go on a journey, who called his own slaves and entrusted his possessions to them. To one he gave five talents, to another, two, and to another, one, each according to his own ability; and he went on his journey. Immediately the one who had received the five talents went and traded with them, and gained five more talents. In the same manner the one who had received the two talents gained two more. But he who received the one talent went away, and dug a hole in the ground and hid his master's money. Now after a long time the master of those slaves came and settled accounts with them. The one who had received the five talents came up and brought five more talents, saying, 'Master, you entrusted five talents to me. See, I have gained five more talents.' His master said to him, 'Well done, good and faithful slave You were faithful with a few things, I will put you in charge of many things; enter into the joy of your master.' Also the one who had received the two talents came up and said, 'Master, you entrusted two talents to me. See, I have gained two more talents.' His master said to him, 'Well done, good and faithful slave. You were faithful with a few things, I will put you in charge of many things; enter into the joy of your master.' And the one also who had received the one talent came up and said, 'Master, I knew you to be a hard man, reaping where you did not sow and gathering where you scattered no seed. And I was afraid, and went away and hid your talent in the ground. See, you have what is yours.' But his master answered and said to him, 'You wicked, lazy slave, you knew that I reap where I did not sow and gather where I scattered no seed. 'Then you ought to have put my money in the bank, and on my arrival I would have received my money back with interest. Therefore take away the talent from him, and give it to the one who has the ten talents.' For to everyone who has, more shall be given, and he will have an abundance; but from the one who does not have, even what he does have shall be taken away. Throw out the worthless slave into the outer darkness; in that place there will be weeping and gnashing of teeth.

Bible verses about prospering

Genesis 26:12
Then Isaac sowed in that land, and reaped in the same year a hundredfold; and the Lord blessed him

Genesis 39:3
Now his master saw that the Lord was with him and how the Lord caused all that he did to prosper in his hand.

Deuteronomy 8:18
...Remember the Lord your God, for it is He who gives you the ability to produce wealth.

Deuteronomy 15:10
You shall generously give to him, and your heart shall not be grieved when you give to him, because for this thing the Lord your God will bless you in all your work and in all your undertakings.

Deuteronomy 24:19
When you reap your harvest in your field and have forgotten a sheaf in the field, you shall not go back to get it; it shall be for the alien, for the orphan, and for the widow, in order that the Lord your God may bless you in all the work of your hands.

Deuteronomy 30:8-10
And you shall again obey the Lord, and observe all His commandments which I command you today. "Then the Lord your God will prosper you abundantly in all the work of your hand, in the offspring of your body and in the offspring of your

cattle and in the produce of your ground, for the Lord will again rejoice over you for good, just as He rejoiced over your fathers; if you obey the Lord your God to keep His commandments and His statutes which are written in this book of the law, if you turn to the Lord your God with all your heart and soul.

Joshua 1:8
This book of the law shall not depart from your mouth, but you shall meditate on it day and night, so that you may be careful to do according to all that is written in it; for then you will make your way prosperous, and then you will have success.

1 Chronicles 22:12
Only may the Lord give you wisdom and understanding, and give you charge concerning Israel, that you may keep the law of the Lord your God. Then you will prosper, if you take care to fulfill the statutes and judgments with which the Lord charged Moses concerning Israel. Be strong and of good courage; do not fear nor be dismayed.

2 Chronicles 31:20
This is what Hezekiah did throughout Judah, doing what was good and right and faithful before the Lord his God. In everything that he undertook in the service of God's temple and in obedience to the law and the commands, he sought his God and worked wholeheartedly. And so he prospered.

Jeremiah 17:8
For he will be like a tree planted by the water, that extends its roots by a stream and will not fear when the heat comes; but its leaves will be green, and it will not be anxious in a year of drought nor cease to yield fruit.

Psalm 1: 1-3

Blessed is the man who does not walk in the counsel of the wicked or stand in the way of sinners or sit in the seat of mockers. But his delight is in the law of the LORD, and on his law he meditates day and night. He is like a tree planted by streams of water, which yields its fruit in season and whose leaf does not wither. Whatever he does prospers.

Psalm 35:27

Let them shout for joy and rejoice, who favor my vindication; and let them say continually, "The Lord be magnified, who delights in the prosperity of His servant."

Malachi 3:10

"Bring all the tithes into the storehouse, that there may be food in My house, And try Me now in this," Says the Lord of hosts, "If I will not open for you the windows of heaven And pour out for you such blessing that there will not be room enough to receive it."

1 Cor 16:2

"On the first day of every week each one of you is to put aside and save, as he may prosper, so that no collections be made when I come."

3 John 1:2

Beloved, I pray that you may prosper in all things and be in health, just as your soul prospers.

Deuteronomy 30:9

The Lord your God will then make you successful in everything you do. He will give you many children and numerous livestock, and he will cause your fields to produce abundant harvests, for the Lord will again delight in being good to you as he was to your ancestors.

Joshua 1:8
This book of the law shall not depart from your mouth, but you shall meditate on it day and night, so that you may be careful to do according to all that is written in it; for then you will make your way prosperous, and then you will have success.

Nehemiah 2:20
…"The God of heaven will give us success; therefore we His servants will arise and build…"

Psalm 1:1-3
Blessed is the man who does not walk in the counsel of the wicked or stand in the way of sinners or sit in the seat of mockers. But his delight is in the law of the Lord, and on his law he meditates day and night. He is like a tree planted by streams of water, which yields its fruit in season and whose leaf does not wither. Whatever he does prospers.

Psalm 37:4
Delight yourself in the Lord; And He will give you the desires of your heart.

Proverbs 22:29
Do you see a man skilled in his work? He will stand before kings; he will not stand before obscure men.

Proverbs 22:4

The reward of humility and the fear of the Lord are riches, honor and life.

Isaiah 1:19

If you consent and obey, you will eat the best of the land;

Matthew 6:24

No one can serve two masters; for either he will hate the one and love the other, or he will be devoted to one and despise the other you cannot serve God and wealth.

Matthew 23:12

Whoever exalts himself shall be humbled; and whoever humbles himself shall be exalted.

Luke 9:48

…and said to them, "Whoever receives this child in My name receives Me, and whoever receives Me receives Him who sent Me; for the one who is least among all of you, this is the one who is great."

Ephesians 3:20

Now to Him who is able to do far more abundantly beyond all that we ask or think, according to the power that works within us.

www.ingramcontent.com/pod-product-compliance
Lightning Source LLC
Chambersburg PA
CBHW051542170526
45165CB00002B/845